Master Your Retirement
How to fulfill your dreams
with peace of mind

Douglas V. Nelson MFA, CFP, CLU

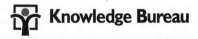

Knowledge Bureau

WINNIPEG, MANITOBA, CANADA

Douglas V. Nelson

MASTER YOUR RETIREMENT
How to fulfill your dreams with peace of mind

ISBN No. 978-1-897526-06-4

Printed and bound in Canada

Canadian Cataloguing in Publication Data

Nelson, Doug, 1967-
    Master your retirement : how to fulfill your dreams with peace of mind / Doug Nelson.

Includes Index

1. Retirement income – Canada – Planning. 2. Finance, Personal – Canada. I. Title.

HG179.N45 2008   332.024'0140971   C2008-908024-6

Publisher:
Knowledge Bureau, Inc.
Box 52042 Niakwa Postal Outlet, Winnipeg, Manitoba Canada R2M 0Z0
204-953-4769 Email: reception@knowledgebureau.com

Research Assistance: Walter Harder and Associates
Editorial Assistance: Norine Harty
Cover and Page Design: Sharon Jones

Acknowledgements

To Karen, Julia, Tamara, Vern and Marian. Thank you so much for your patience, love and encouragement. I truly love what I do and I am grateful that you support me in my efforts. I am one lucky guy. I love you all.

Knowledge Bureau
CANADA'S LEADING EDUCATOR IN TAX AND FINANCIAL SERVICES

Presents
Financial Education for Decision Makers

The Master Your Personal Finances Books:

Master Your Taxes
How to maximize your after-tax returns

Master Your Retirement
How to fulfill your dreams with peace of mind

Master Your Investment in the Family Business
How to increase after-tax wealth

Master Your Money Management
How to manage the advisors who work for you

Master Your Real Wealth
How to live your life with financial security

FREE
UPDATING
SERVICES

Keep up your Mastery! For the latest in tax and personal financial planning strategies subscribe to Breaking Tax and Investment News. Visit www.knowledgebureau.com/masteryourtaxes

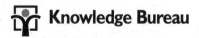

Knowledge Bureau

Knowledge Bureau Newsbooks are available at special discounts to use as sales promotions or for advisor/corporate training programs. For more information, address a query to Manager, Business Development at The Knowledge Bureau:
reception@knowledgebureau.com
1-866-953-4769
www.knowledgebureau.com

Contents

Introduction

Understanding the New Triggers
and Phases of Retirement

According to the last Canadian Census (2006):

- The average age in Canada in 2008 was age 52. There were more 52 year olds than any other age group.
- The baby boom demographic represents 30% of the population in Canada. This group represents those born between 1946 and 1966.
- In 2011, the first of the baby boomers reach 65. As this baby boom demographic ages, the growth of the elderly population will accelerate considerably. This will bring about far reaching changes to our economy and your investments.
- Seniors in Canada will outnumber children by 2018.
- In 2008, the average life expectancy of Canadians, which increased appreciably over the past century, was 82.5 years for women and 77.7 years for men, resulting in more reaching age 65 and living longer after.

This book, therefore is for the average 50-something baby boomer and his or her parents. If you are on the younger side of that demographic, the next 30 or so years of your life will be an interesting ride. For everyone else, let's face it, retirement is certainly not going to be anything like it used to be!

What are the triggers for retirement? What is going to make you stop and think and plan for it? Lifestyle? Life's work? Life's end? Healthy, active, busy and engaged people are often not ready to think about their transition into retirement, but they need to, especially against a backdrop of unpredictable financial times and a host of real personal factors. Those in retirement now, may need to rethink and replan, for the same reasons.

You might be surprised to know that of the 7.4 million people in Canada aged 55 and over, 63.7% (that's close to 5 million people) had already retired…at least once! These people initially retired for several different reasons:

- 23.7% due to personal and family responsibilities.
- 22.8% due to personal health concerns.
- Only 19.6% retired because they now qualified for a full pension.

In short, as much as you may think you are in control of you future, the reality is that only 20% of those who retired in the last several years did so because they could. *Over 45% of Canadians who did retire did so for reasons beyond their control.*

In fact, many who will retire will return to work. Of the above group, close to 50% return to some form of work for financial reasons; while others returned to work due to the availability of new, interesting and inspiring job offers.

All of this information illustrates the fact that no two retirements are alike. Virtually every retirement is unique based on the jobs, incomes, pensions, ages, preferences, abilities, health, priorities and interests. To add to this complexity is the fact that both spouses in today's modern age have typically had an income and typically have some form of retirement assets. Therefore, you need to plan for "two" retirements today and not just one.

For example:

- Each spouse or partner may retire at the same time.
- Each spouse may retire at different times.

- One may retire many years before the other due to a significant difference in age.
- One may wish to travel and volunteer time in the community while the other may wish to stay at home and putter in the yard.
- One may wish to do whatever possible to retire from a stressful current work environment, while the other may have significant retirement goals and plans and can't wait to begin to act on these plans.
- One may be forced to retire gradually, or all at once, due to health issues. The other spouse may wish to retire sooner than planned due to the health care needs of another family member.
- One may retire for a short period of time, only to go back to work again on a part time basis. The other may retire for a short period of time, only to start a small business a few years into retirement.

Retirement can mean different things to different people, none of which are wrong or inappropriate, they are just different. There are literally thousands of possible combinations of events or stages that you and your spouse may find throughout your retirement years. As a matter of fact, there are Five Key Phases to Every Retirementt, and each comes with different personal triggers.

Phase 1: The Pre-Retirement Years

This is typically the three to five years before you are completely finished working. You may work part time during this phase and gradually transition to full time retirement living. For some this period may be between the ages of 50 and 55, while for others it may be between the ages of 70 and 75. The difference in the ages may have nothing to do with money. Rather, it may have everything to do with lifestyle desires and the personal satisfaction that comes from work. When it comes to retirement there is no right or wrong and the answers to your questions may not be black and white. Rather, the right answers for you are based on your own personal preferences and comfort zone. Continue to do whatever you enjoy and do your best to avoid the stereotypes that suggest what you should or should not be doing at this stage in life.

Phase 2: The First Two Years

The first two years of full retirement is a period of significant adjustment. During this time you will gain a better understanding of your basic income needs as well as your lifestyle wants. In the previous phase you created some projections of what you were expecting to happen. Now you are able to compare your projections with real life experiences. You will also begin to forge a new routine. The relationship between you and your spouse may evolve significantly during this time or you may find yourself going through a rough patch. You will begin to sort out activities you wish to do on your own and those you wish to do together. You will spend more time with others who are of a similar age and doing the same type of activities. You may do things that you never thought you'd do.

In this phase it is tempting for many to make some big decisions, the most common of which has to do with your home. Be patient during this time and do not make any significant decisions. The First Two Years is a time for adjustment, trial and error and reflection. What you thought you may want to do in retirement may very well change during these first two years. The people you thought you'd spend time with may also change. It is be prudent to resist the temptation to rush into any big decisions. This is a time to try as many different things as possible. Much will change in the first two years of retirement, so "let the dust settle" and don't make any big decisions at this time unless absolutely necessary.

Phase 3: The Active Years

The retired individual or couple often has the greatest clarity and drive during this phase. People are clear as to what they wish to do, where they wish to go, and with whom they wish to spend time. During this time the couple is very active, often more active and busy than during the working years. They are very focused, determined and purposeful in how they spend their time. In many situations the couple shares a sense of urgency for certain priorities. Life is active, healthy and vibrant. For some this may be a period of time that lasts 10 to 15 years while for others it may only be one to two years. When planning for this stage, keep in mind the age of your children and grandchildren. You can easily project the ages and life activities of the loved ones around you and with this information in mind you can plan your own active lifestyle with confidence and enthusiasm.

Phase 4: When Illness Strikes

As we age, changes occur in our bodies and our minds. New aches and pains begin to set in making it more and more difficult to do the things you most wish to do. In more serious situations the illness requires invasive surgery, perhaps months of hospital treatments and/or a new regimen of daily medications. This phase will inevitably transition one spouse to the roll of caregiver, adding considerable fatigue and financial hardship on the healthy spouse, especially if the final diagnosis is a long term debilitating disease. Watching your lifelong friend, lover and partner go through such an illness can be extremely agonizing and stressful. This stress may also transition to the extended family. One day you may even find that the "healthy" spouse is just not able to keep up with the needs of the spouse with the illness. At this time the discussion takes place of moving one, or both, to a more suitable housing facility. This is a period in time that could last weeks, months or even a decade.

Phase 5: When You are on Your Own Again

A final phase of retirement for many is the time spent on their own after the death of their spouse. For some this may be a period of 10 to 20 years, while for others it may be a matter of months. In some situations, the surviving spouse may now be in charge of certain areas of his or her life that he or she has never had to deal with in the past. A common example of this is the finances. If the individual who handled the finances of the household is the one who passes away first, the surviving spouse can often find these new responsibilities to be very intimidating. The decisions that need to be made after the death of a spouse can be daunting, while the decisions regarding the final transition of your assets to your beneficiaries may create even more stress, fatigue and insecurity.

THE TEN STEPS

Though every retirement is different, there are ten specific steps that you can take every one to three years to truly *Master Your Retirement*. These 10 steps are discussed in detail throughout the book. For your reference, here they are in simple terms.

1. **Always start with your vision:** Project your lifestyle vision and milestones for the next three to five years. This vision will include all aspects of your life, your health and your relationships. Continue to update your vision every 12 to 36 months.

2. **Identify your income needs and wants:** Project your basic income needs for the next few years and match this up with guaranteed sources of income. Project your lifestyle income wants and match this up, to the extent you desire, with your variable sources of income.

3. **Understand your changing Financial Risk Profile:** Update your Financial Risk Profile and ensure that your current investment portfolio and way of life is always consistent with this profile. Be true to yourself and do not take any unnecessary risks.

4. **Balance the income and growth potential of your investment portfolio with your lifestyle vision and income needs:** Measure the income and growth potential of your current investment portfolio based on your risk profile and your income needs. Are your income needs greater than the income you expect to receive from the portfolio? Will you need to take more risk to achieve your income benchmark? If these are not in balance then you will need to make some changes to either your income needs or the structure of your portfolio. Whatever you do, don't compromise on your risk profile (i.e. don't take more risk that what you are comfortable with taking, this will likely only backfire on you).

5. **Manage your tax:** Measure the tax efficiency of your income for the current year and for the next three to five years. Make sure you are staying within the clawback zones and receiving as an efficient amount of income as possible. Make modifications to your investment portfolio and other sources of income as possible to meet your tax efficiency objectives.

6. **Measure your health care risks:** As you enter "the illness phase" one of you may need ongoing home care or facility care. This can be extremely expensive. If this happened in the next three to five years, what would you do and what would be the financial impact? Spend time to consider these possibilities and make informed decisions as to the best future course of action.

7. **Measure the survivor risks:** Ultimately, one partner will be left on their own. What if this happens in the next three to five years? What will you do and what will be the financial impact? Spend time to consider these possibilities and make informed decisions as to the best future course of action.

8. **Measure the final estate outcome:** As you and your spouse end your life's journey, how will your final affairs be wound up and what will be the implications? Will family harmony be intact? Will taxes be minimized? What will be your lasting legacy?

9. **Take action:** Update your Will, Power of Attorney, Living Will (health care directive), investment portfolio, and your life and health insurance as necessary to meet your objectives.

10. **Communicate:** Share all of these issues with your family; it is important that they are aware of your plans.

The Benefits

By following each of these 10 steps, reviewing them every one to three years and being aware of the Five Phases of Retirement, you will truly Master Your Retirement. You will:

- adapt to changing circumstances easily,
- reap the benefits of tax efficiency,
- live the life you most desire to have,
- sleep comfortably at night knowing your portfolio has the right risk profile and your basic income needs will always be met,
- pro-actively plan your future,
- leave nothing to chance,
- avoid family conflicts and miscommunication,
- maximize your lasting legacy for generations to come.

IN SUMMARY

To Master Your Retirement is to picture your retirement three years at a time and know you have made plans for all aspects of your life: career, physical activity, health, your spouse, your family and your other relationships. Having a plan you are excited about is one of the great contributors to longevity, health and happiness. This is just one of the key differences between people who just "do" retirement, and those who "MASTER" retirement.

THE FORMAT OF THIS BOOK

The Principles for Mastering Your Retirement are discussed in this book in a straight forward fashion, with common features to empower you. In each chapter you will find:

- *A True to Life Scenario:* These feature fictitious families in real-life situations as a backdrop for the principles discussed in the chapter.
- *The Issues:* What is important and why?
- *The Solutions:* What do you need to know to make the right financial decisions for your time and money? How can you best integrate these solutions in your strategic plan to meet goals by asking the right questions?
- *The Mastery:* Tips and Traps to help you put your financial decision making into focus, simplify your efforts, and get better results.

We hope you will find this format fruitful in taking control and making better financial decisions, either on your own, or together with your team of financial advisors.

DOUG NELSON AND
THE KNOWLEDGE BUREAU

CHAPTER 1

Ready? Set? Or Are We?

When you can't have what you want, it's time to start wanting what you have. KATHLEEN A. SUTTON

Robert and Elizabeth are both turning 60 this year and are planning to retire, but they have many questions. What will they do? Where will they live? Will they get along? Will they have enough money? Are they ready? These are the most common questions facing everyone as they approach retirement.

Robert is ready to retire. He has worked for the same company and in the same department for the past 25 years. He is tired of the day to day grind and is ready to leave it all behind. He can't wait to retire.

Elizabeth, on the other hand, is quite unsure about retirement. While she can relate to Robert's eagerness for a different life, she is concerned that a) their investments have not performed as expected and they do not have enough money to retire, b) they will feel anxious seeing their income fluctuate as the value of their portfolio fluctuates, c) once they retire they may become "old" before their time and d) she and Robert will have trouble finding things to do for the next 20 years of their life.

Robert and Elizabeth have worked hard their entire lives and are ready to enjoy the fruits of their labour. At this time the grass seems to be greener on the retirement side of the fence, but is it really? Are they more excited about leaving the work force than they are about their future lifestyle?

THE ISSUES

Are Robert and Elizabeth ready to retire "financially"?

Are Robert and Elizabeth ready to retire "psychologically"?

These are two completely different issues.

Are they looking forward to the same things or do they each have a different vision of retirement? Does each one know what is important to the other?

The extent to which both spouses are in sync with the other in terms of the ideal retirement vision is extremely important. This does not mean both spouses need to spend every waking moment together doing the same thing. Actually, for many it is quite the opposite. A shared vision for retirement is a very important issue. A shared vision for retirement identifies matters that are important to both spouses and also includes recognition of the vision of each spouse individually. This shared vision will help to avoid misunderstandings while also providing the opportunity for each spouse to support the other in those activities.

What will be the plan for today and how does this compare with the longer term plan? What should the plan include? How far in the future should they plan?

A plan for retirement must include many components. These components are similar to what you need today to enjoy your life to the fullest. The plan includes health, activities and relationships. When developing your plan for retirement, it is very important to consider each of these components, both over the short term and the long term.

How important is it to have as many "guarantees" as possible throughout their retirement years? Having a vision and a plan is one thing, having a realistic, low risk plan is something else. Keeping your risks low in retirement is very important.

Are you **Ready**? Are you **Set** in your plans? Or is something holding you back?

To resolve the questions that are in your mind today, you must first develop a vision for what your ideal retirement, for the next three to five years in particular, will look like. This vision should be reviewed and discussed, ideally, every one to three years.

THE SOLUTIONS

Retirement is a new phase of life, perhaps a phase that is unlike any you have experienced before. This is scary for some and exciting for others. This is a time and place in which some cannot wait to arrive, while it is something that others insist on postponing as long as possible. Some will enjoy retirement, some will excel at retirement and others will fail miserably. As you know with all things in life, it is ultimately up to you to decide your own level of success. Your level of success will depend on how well you prepare for this new phase of life and how well you adapt along the way.

This book was written to help you become a "Master" of your retirement, living this time to your fullest, regardless of your health, your abilities or your finances.

I want you to look back on this time, and on your life, as a period of great joy, fulfillment, achievement and satisfaction. When your retirement period ends, I want you to be at peace with yourself, your family, your community and with the world. If this has occurred, you have created a lasting legacy of memories, you have passed on the stories of your life, you have passed on your wisdom and you have perhaps even shared your financial resources for the benefit and empowerment of others. Is this a lofty goal? Perhaps, but when you think of it, should the goal be anything less?

What makes this period so incredible is the fact that some or all of your income will come from sources other than work! You will be part of less than 10% of the world's population who live a life without having to work! How fortunate you are! How blessed you are! Not only will you have the chance to live a life without having to work, but you may do so over a period of time that could be the longest and most significant part of your life!

Now let's build a compelling vision of your "ideal" retired life going forward by discussing:

1. What is a retirement vision?
2. How do you create a vision for retirement?
3. What should this vision include?
4. Why can transitioning to retirement be so challenging?
5. How do you know if you are ready to retire?

WHAT IS A RETIREMENT VISION?

Very simply, a retirement vision is a picture of your ideal life moving forward. This picture is extremely important for several reasons:

- Many people are unsure if they will be happy in retirement. The only way to know if you will be happy is to have a picture in your mind of what your ideal retirement period will look like.

- Retirement is a long period of time with as many as five different phases. To be happy in retirement it is extremely important to anticipate and plan for these phases. People are unhappy in retirement when they are ill prepared for these phases and an unexpected crisis, illness or death occurs.

- A vision for retirement helps to identify the expenses you will have. By identifying the expenses, you will be able to determine the income you will require.

- A vision is important because it will help you to retire "to" something important and meaningful to you. Alternatively, some people can't wait to retire from their current job. In these instances they are retiring "from" something. If you are retiring "from" something rather than "to" something, you may find your level of happiness is much less than what you thought it would be. A vision is extremely important to provide interest, excitement and meaning to your retirement.

HOW TO CREATE A VISION FOR RETIREMENT

To create a unique and compelling vision for retirement, you will need to follow three important steps:

1. Make a list of The Top 100 things that are most important to you.
2. Plot this list onto a "Lifeline" chart that shows the incremental time between today and the day you die.
3. Set some goals. Make sure you cover all of the important aspects of your vision: your health, your relationships and your activities.

Now let's take a look at each of these steps in more detail.

The Top 100

Make a list of all the things you'd love to do before you die. A recent movie has referred to this as the "Bucket List", the things you'd love to do before you "kick the bucket". Try to list as many things as you can such as:

- The places you'd love to see.
- The things you'd love to do.
- The people you'd like to visit.
- The number of times you'd like to have the grandkids over for a sleepover.
- The number of days each year you'd like to spend at the lake.
- New things you'd like to learn.
- Relationships you'd like to mend.
- Problems you'd like to solve.
- Things you'd like to do on your own.

- Things you'd like to do with your spouse.
- Contributions you'd like to make (to the community).
- Time you'd like to volunteer.

If the list is full you will never be short of ideas. Do this on your own and then with your spouse. Compare your lists and set some priorities.

The Lifeline

This next step takes the list of things you identified in your 100 list and begins to set some time frames. For example:

- Draw a line from left to right on a large piece of paper. The far left end of the line is where you are today. This is the point in time where you are at today in your life.
- Write down your name and your age on the far left end of the line.
- Now take a look at the far right end of the line. The far right end of the line will be the day you die. For the sake of discussion enter age 85 on the far right end of the line. This represents the age in which you will pass away.
- This leaves us the space in between the far left and the far right, the space between today and the day you die. The space in between is the time available to do all of the 100 things you'd like to do before you die.
- Now fill in the gaps between where you are today (on the far left) and the age you noted on the right end of the line. Mark a spot on the line for every three year period. If you are 60 today create a point on the life line for ages 63, 66, 69, 72, 75, 78, 82 and 85.
- Enter your age above each three year increment.
- Now begin to fill in the spaces under each three year increment. Enter those places you'd like to see, activities you'd like to do, people you'd like to spend time with and things you'd like to learn. Try to enter everything on your Top 100 List. If you can't enter everything, then determine which items on the Top 100 List are most important.

- When you see your "lifeline" you will begin to develop the "ideal" vision for your life from this point forward. If this vision is exciting to you, then you know you are on the right track. If it is not exciting to you, then make the necessary changes.

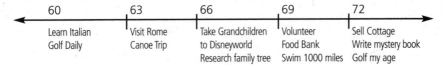

60	63	66	69	72
Learn Italian	Visit Rome	Take Grandchildren	Volunteer	Sell Cottage
Golf Daily	Canoe Trip	to Disneyworld	Food Bank	Write mystery book
		Research family tree	Swim 1000 miles	Golf my age

By following these steps you have painted a picture of what you will do with your time at each stage of your life moving forward. Seeing the time slip away across the lifeline can be very sobering and create a very compelling sense of urgency.

Take what you have done to the next level:

- Enter the name and age of your spouse over these same periods of time.
- Do this again for your children and your grandchildren.

What do you see? Will you change the timing and urgency of some of your own activities due to the ages of others? In most situations the answer will be "yes". When you begin to take into account the age of others, your lifeline vision will most definitely change. When your oldest grandchild is 25 will he prefer a trip to Disneyworld or another location?

Now look at the overall lifeline one more time. How does it look? Are you excited? Is this the picture of your ideal life moving forward? Do you and your spouse share the same vision? If not, where are the compromises?

Set Some Goals

It is now time to make sure you have set some goals in all of the most important areas of your life.

- **Your health:** You see from this vision just how important it will be to have your health over time. If you are planning on being active throughout your 70's and into your 80's, a healthy diet with regular exercise is critical to your ability to live out your ideal vision. As you reflect on your "lifeline" thus far, make some notes underneath and perhaps at every interval stating your health and exercise related goals.

- **Your relationships:** You may dedicate space on your lifeline for activities and time spent enhancing your relationship(s) and/or repairing broken relationships. When your relationships are intact, you are often having the most fun and you are the most at peace. When relationships are broken and conflict persists, it is easy to be muddled, de-energized, isolated and miserable. Therefore, when building an ideal vision it is important and valuable to commit time on your lifeline to enhance your relationships.

- **Your activities:** Make a list of the regular activities you'd like to participate in each year. This is also extremely important and beneficial. This may include sporting activities that you participate in at various times throughout each year, hobbies or volunteer activities in the community. You may wish to continue to work part time for several years or run a small business or do some extra consulting work. All of these are examples of the things you will be doing to keep busy, interested and engaged in the world around you.

- **Your milestones:** Milestones will be specific dates or points in time when specific events will take place. For example, high school or university graduation (kids and grandkids), marriage dates or dates in which your income may change for one reason or another.

At the end of this process you have created a line marked by three year increments. Above this line will be the names and ages of the people closest to you. Below this line may be several rows. The first row may be your "Top 100". The next row may be your health list. The next row may be your relationships list. The next row may be your activities list. The next row may be your list of milestones.

By following these steps you have created a very compelling vision of your life going forward. Sit back and take some time to live with this vision. How does it make you feel? What would you change? If you could add anything, what would you add? If you could take anything away, what would you take away?

OTHER BIG RETIREMENT DECISIONS

When mapping out your vision, consider the following issues:

- **Should you retire all at once or should you retire gradually?** For many people, work helps to bring meaning, purpose and a sense of fulfillment to life. Work in and of itself may not be the issue for you, rather, it may be the type of work you do or the amount of work you do. If you were in control of your time and your work, would you be more satisfied with your life? Would you make more money? If you answered yes, perhaps you will want to think about retiring gradually over time. Perhaps you do not need to stop working at all, all you need is to gain control over your work.

  In 2008, a provision became available for people who are members of a defined benefit pension plan in Canada which gives the option today of receiving some pension income while still working part time for the same company and continuing to contribute to the same pension plan. If you had this type of guaranteed basic income coming in month after month, would that change the way you view your work, your time and your life?

- **Should you and your spouse retire at the same time?** As mentioned earlier, you are planning for the retirement of not just one individual, but for two. You may choose to retire today while your spouse may choose to retire in a few years time. This may be an excellent consideration since the additional employment income will give you and your spouse opportunities to do the things you most want to do in the early years of retirement.

- **Should you sell your business?** Many small to mid sized businesses produce a significant amount of cash flow. This cash flow can give the owner(s) an above average income month after month. If the business were sold, the net proceeds after tax may not be enough to replace this income. It is important to weigh the financial implications of keeping the business alive or selling it outright today. In many cases the business as a long term going concern is worth more to the retiree then it is if it were wound down or sold.

WHY CAN IT BE CHALLENGING TO TRANSITION TO RETIREMENT?

To truly Master Your Retirement, it is extremely important to understand why transitioning to retirement can be such a challenge. If you understand the challenges then you can prepare to address these challenges in advance.

- **Retirement is a long period of time:** Retirement may be 15 to 25 years in length, and many people find it difficult to fathom what they would do over such a long period of time. By working through each of the three steps in the retirement vision process noted previously in this chapter, and by understanding the Five Phases of Retirement, you begin to realize that this period of time can go by very quickly. The retirement vision process is your best approach to create a compelling vision of your life and a strong sense of urgency.

- **Retirement, for some, may be viewed as the beginning of the end:** For many people retirement is viewed as just one step closer to the grave yard. Due to this fear of death, some people give up on life completely. They assume that tomorrow will be their last, so there is no point in starting anything new today. To overcome this fear, go back to your retirement vision and assume that you will live longer than you expect. Yes, you must plan for longevity. By planning for longevity you will be creating a long list of all of the things that are important to you. By creating this list you will also create a keen sense of urgency to get through this list.

- **Retirement means sickness:** It is difficult, if not impossible, to ignore the fact that life is drawing to an end. With every new ache or pain it is impossible not to think in terms of cancer, heart disease or stroke. Yet, ironically, the more one ponders about life's great ailments, the more they can become self-fulfilling outcomes. Before you know it, time has passed and opportunities have been missed. If death and disease is something that pre-occupies your thoughts, perhaps you should approach life with a greater sense of urgency. It is also best to do a financial audit to prepare for when illness strikes. In the introduction we referred to this as "Measuring Your Health Care Risks". By doing this work you will begin to alleviate your fears in this area and help you move forward. Don't let health issues distract you. Confront them.

- **Your employment income ends:** For the first time in your life your income will come from sources other than "work". Your entire income will now come from your investments, pensions and government benefits. It can be extremely difficult for some to adjust to this new reality. It can be extremely difficult to "trust" that your income will always be there. This is often a huge source of stress for many couples in retirement. To rely on investment returns from this point forward can often create more fear than certainty because of the complexity of the investment world and the often scary fluctuations of the stock market. In this book I will present to you a concept I refer to as the 100% Guaranteed Solution. If you are nervous about your income, there are many ways available to create more certainty, as you will see later in this book.

- **Retirement changes your sense of who you are:** Retirement can be difficult because you stop working? Ironic, isn't it? You strive to get to a time and place when you no longer have to work, yet stopping work may result in more stress. Work gives a sense of accomplishment, a sense of contribution, a sense of usefulness and, for many, a sense of who you are. For most of our lives, our sense of identity is defined by education, career, job title or the nature of our business. While raising a family your identity may also be linked to the activities of your children or by the community in which you live.

Yet, when you retire both your work identity and your parental identity may diminish or cease to exist. Who are you as you enter this next phase of life? Who are you without your kids? Who are you without your job? Who are you without your business? When you retire your sense of identity will shift. Getting your mind around this shift in identity may take some time.

- **Personal satisfaction may not come from retirement:** Rather it may come from control related issues. Many people believe that work is what we need to get away from, when in fact, "work" in itself is not really the problem. The real challenge is to have control of your time, your destiny and to have the choice to do what you want when you want. Some form of work or meaningful activity is vital to happiness and overall retirement success. For those who do not recognize this reality, retirement may be extremely difficult. It is therefore important to consider all of your options. Maybe the best approach is to gradually retire over time?

- **Are you healthy enough to enjoy retirement?** At this time of life your energy, your health and your physical strength is not what it has been in the past. To fully master this time of life, attention to your physical health is of utmost importance. Without a reasonable amount of good health, you may find that you will begin to miss out on gatherings and activities with family and friends. This can result in the feeling of isolation and resentment that can in turn create greater negative health effects Spending time reflecting on your health, your activities and your relationships is just as important as reflecting on your investments and different sources of income.

HOW DO YOU KNOW IF YOU ARE READY TO RETIRE?

The best answer to this question comes from your retirement vision. Is the vision compelling, meaningful, exciting and energizing? If so, then you know that you are truly retiring "to" something rather than just retiring "from" something.

When you think of retirement, do you think of "just getting by" or can you get excited about "mastering" your retirement? Can you look forward to doing something new? Or are you just focused on getting away from what ails you today?

If you answered positively to these questions, you are psychologically ready for retirement. Remember, even though you may feel that you are ready to retire, this readiness should not be driven by how tired or frustrated you are today with the daily grind. Odds are that retirement will bring its own challenges and frustrations. To see your way through these inevitable challenges, it is critical to have your goals, your dreams, your vision and your passions clearly identified.

Are you financially ready to retire? To answer this question, allow me to pose other questions:

- Were you financially ready to buy your first home?
- Were you financially ready to be married?
- Were you financially ready to start a family?
- Were you financially ready to have your children attend university?

I think you get my point. I believe that most people will never "think" they have enough money to retire, regardless of how much wealth they really have. Therefore, the purpose of this book is to teach you how to make sure your overall after-tax income is as large and as safe as possible. We focus on after-tax income because it does not matter what you have, it only matters what you keep.

IN SUMMARY

THINGS YOU NEED TO KNOW

- You will know that you are truly ready to retire when you have a clear "vision" of what your retirement will look like.
- To Master Your Retirement, find a balance between your health, your relationships and your activities.
- The financial objective is to maximize after-tax income by minimizing income taxes. This issue alone can have great impact on Mastering Your Retirement.
- You will never think you have enough money to retire. You will always feel you need more.

QUESTIONS YOU NEED TO ASK

- Are you retiring "from" a bad situation at work OR are you retiring "to" a clear vision and journey that you are excited to embark upon?
- If you had more control over your working environment, would this influence how and when you retire?
- Do you "need" to continue to work so as to feel that you are remaining active and involved in the community or for your own enjoyment?
- Do you and your spouse have a different vision of retirement?
- What do you need to do to find the ideal compromise?

THINGS YOU NEED TO DO

- Follow the three step retirement vision process.
  1. Begin making a list of your Top 100.
  2. Begin to map out your Lifeline.
  3. Think of your future in terms of health, activities, relationships and milestones.
- Have your spouse complete the same three steps and compare your answers.

DECISIONS YOU NEED TO MAKE

- What is my retirement vision? My spouse's vision? How do we combine these two visions?
- What are my goals for retirement?
- Should I retire gradually?
- Should my spouse and I both retire at the same time?

MASTER YOUR RETIREMENT
Ready? Set? Or Are We?

TIPS

- Creating a vision for your retirement is the most important step to determine if you are ready to retire, if your retirement will be a success and to determine if you have enough money to retire.
- The Top 100 List and the Lifeline approach are two proven methods to help build your vision for retirement.
- It is extremely important to retire "to" something rather than retire "from" something.
- Your vision should always include specific strategies to address your health needs, your relationships, your levels of activity and your milestones.
- No two retirements are alike.

TRAPS

- You and your spouse may approach retirement in your own unique way. Give each other the latitude to do so, plan your individual retirements as well as your retirement together. Forcing your vision of retirement on your spouse is a trap you should definitely avoid.
- There are many different options for retirement including retiring gradually, working part time and starting a small business. Your retirement vision is unique to you and it can be whatever you want it to be. Don't get stuck in thinking that there is only one vision or perspective on retirement.
- Some people struggle with retirement because it can be a very long period of time. Their identity will shift, they will fear aging and illness, they will have a fear of running out of money and they will fear the volatility of their investment portfolio. Recognize these realities in advance and don't fall into the trap of being fearful of them.
- It is critically important to find a good balance between your health,

relationships and finances in retirement. If you become pre-occupied with only your finances, for example, you may find that you are never able to fully enjoy your health or your relationships.

• To truly Master Your Retirement, plan your ideal life three to five years at a time. Never put off for tomorrow what you can do today.

Principle Mastery: As the saying goes "failing to plan ahead" is akin to "planning to fail". Transitioning into retirement is one of the most significant events of your life. Take the time necessary to build a clear vision and you will be rewarded with greater health, closer relationships and a more fulfilling life.

CHAPTER 2

A Lifetime of Abundance, Choice, Low Risk and Guaranteed Income: A Dream Come True

When we are motivated by goals that have deep meaning, by dreams that need completion, by pure love that needs expressing—then we truly live life.
GREG ANDERSON

Mark and Joanne are ready to retire. They are very clear as to how they will spend the next two to five years of their retirement. They are very excited about the things they will be doing, the places they will be going and the people they will be spending time with along the way.

Mark and Joanne have calculated that if they could have a consistent investment return of 8% to 10% per year, they would be able to achieve their retirement dreams. While they can put up with some fluctuations in rate of return, if there was a year of negative return they would have to significantly adjust their lifestyle going forward.

Their retirement vision is clear, their goals are specific and they are focused on an abundant full life today and in the years ahead.

Yet, are Mark and Joanne's goals realistic? Should they stake their quality of life in retirement on a target rate of return? Is their rate of return target a reasonable expectation? Are Mark and Joanne unknowingly taking on too much risk? Do their retirement plans and goals match their overall comfort with risk? How should Mark and Joanne best proceed to answer these questions?

THE ISSUES

Now that you have created an overall vision for retirement, the next step is to deliver that vision in a manner that is as low risk as possible. I have yet to meet anyone who wanted to take on more risk in their retirement. Yet, what creates the most havoc for most retirees are situations or scenarios that catch them off guard.

A simple example of this relates to the investment markets. Many investors will say things like, "I didn't realize that what I was investing in had such a high risk." Usually, this statement is made only after the investment they were holding produced a significant negative return.

How can you find your ideal risk level? Start with a "benchmark", a standard to compare the other alternatives against. As the saying goes, "everything is relative", if you don't have a framework in which to make a comparison, then it is very difficult to make an informed decision.

When we look at retirement planning, we need to create benchmarks for investment risk and return, income guarantees and taxation. Without these benchmarks you run the risk of being easily influenced by the next great investment idea or product concept.

When assessing risk and return, there are many issues to consider:

- What is a reasonable long term investment return to consider when planning and forecasting your retirement?
- How much risk do you have to accept to achieve this return?
- How do you know if you are comfortable with this much risk?
- How much of your retirement income should you put at risk?
- Would you prefer a 100% guaranteed income solution?
- What other financial risks could confront you in retirement?
- Is an 8% to 10% consistent return with minimal risk a reasonable expectation?
- Is your entire retirement vision dependent on the returns in your portfolio?
- What are the greatest risks to a lifetime of abundance, choice, and guaranteed income?

- What source of income should you draw from first? How should you structure retirement income so that it is safe and guaranteed?

- What is an ideal benchmark in which to measure your plan for income?

THE SOLUTIONS

Understanding Risk and Return

What is a reasonable rate of return and how much risk does one have to take to achieve this return? Ironically, at the time of writing this book we are experiencing a substantial market decline. These declines do occur and the timing of one's retirement date is critical. First and foremost, it is extremely important to know that those who retire at the beginning of a market cycle have substantially greater odds of financial success than one who retires at the end of a market cycle. The year 2000 is considered to be the end of the last growth cycle. The period between 2000 - 2008 or even to 2015 is considered to be a bear market or sideways market cycle. Those who retire during this period of time need to be cautious. During times like these consider the value of guaranteed, low risk approaches such as the 100% guaranteed solution discussed later in this chapter.

Let's look at what some of the long term averages tell us. A Balanced Portfolio, one that invests 50% in Canadian Bonds and 50% in Canadian stocks, over the last 25 years has seen an annual compound return of 8%. By comparison, the Canadian stock market has seen an annual compound return of 10.1%. With this in mind, is an 8% return reasonable? Over a long period of time, an 8% return has been produced, but to get this return you will have had to endure substantial risk. For example, some years the Balanced Portfolio has seen annual returns as low as -18%. This would clearly not do for Mark and Joanne.

If you are retired and drawing a regular income from your investments, and the value of those investments drop, you may never recover the money you have lost. If the value of your portfolio is $500,000 and you are drawing 8% per year (i.e.: $40,000) and the value of your portfolio drops by just 10%, the value of your portfolio at the end of the year would range between $410,000 (if you took out all of your income at the beginning of the year) and $432,000 (if you took out the income gradually throughout the year). To receive $40,000 in income the next year after, the portfolio will now need to earn 9.25% to 9.75% per year from this point forward just to maintain your income. To receive this higher rate of return, you will need to change your portfolio from balanced to an extremely high risk structure by investing 100% of your portfolio in the stock market.

One of the ways to measure risk is by using something called "standard deviation". Standard deviation measures the volatility of investment returns over a period of time. As an example, let's assume that we wish to compare the pros and cons of investment A vs. investment B. The long term average annual rate of return for each is 8%. The question is, how much risk did you have to take with Investment A to achieve the 8% return vs. how much risk did you have to take with Investment B to achieve the same 8% return. The standard deviation tells us how much volatility occurred in both Investment A and Investment B. The higher the standard deviation, the higher the level of risk. Therefore, you would want to choose the investment with the lower standard deviation.

The difference in the level of standard deviation (i.e.: risk) between the balanced portfolio and the Toronto Stock Exchange is a whopping 75%. In other words, to increase the average rate of return from 8% to 10% you will need to increase the level of risk and volatility by 75%!

Every investment has some risk. Investors need to be careful NOT to be lulled into a false sense of belief that high annual returns are the norm. Investors must always be aware of the downside risks to a portfolio. It will be the one or two bad years that can quickly undo 4 to 5 good years. That is why you need to pay more attention to risk than return.

What is a reasonable long term return expectation? Based on historical data, to be conservative use a range from 4% to 6%.

HOW MUCH OF YOUR RETIREMENT VISION SHOULD YOU PUT AT RISK?

With this basic understanding of risk and volatility, to what extent do you wish to have your retirement income exposed to investments that in the past have declined by as much as 10% to 18%? An investment portfolio provides a variable source of income due to the fact that the returns from year to year may vary greatly.

If this is a concern to you, then the next question is: to what extent do you wish to have at least your basic monthly expenses covered by guaranteed sources of income?

To determine the amount of your retirement vision that is at risk, you need to follow these steps:

a) Identify and make a list of your various sources of income.

b) Identify which sources of income are guaranteed and which are variable.

c) Make a list of your various expenses and break them down into monthly or annual expenses.

d) Go through the list of expenses and identify each expense as either a "basic income need" or as an "enhanced lifestyle want". The basic income needs represent your basic costs of living. Your lifestyle wants represent the travel, golf memberships, and other entertainment dollars that you spend.

To determine the extent to which your retirement vision is at risk, first and foremost, your basic income needs should be covered by guaranteed sources of income to ensure your basic lifestyle is not impacted by fluctuations in the economy or in your portfolio. If your enhanced lifestyle wants are funded by your variable investments, you have the option of cutting back on these wants should you need to do so.

How much of your retirement vision should you put at risk? The answer will be different for everyone. To create a benchmark, however, follow the steps noted above to give you a reasonable amount of security and peace of mind. You will have the flexibility to curb your discretionary spending, while your guaranteed sources of income will cover your basic needs.

How much of your retirement vision should you put at risk to fluctuating markets? Perhaps the answer to this question for you is zero. For others is may be 10%, 20% or 30% of total income or the answer may be found in the relationship between basic income needs and enhanced lifestyle wants. It is important to resolve this question to give you peace of mind in retirement.

THE SEVEN MOST CRITICAL RISKS TO A LIFETIME OF ABUNDANCE, CHOICE, LOW RISK AND GUARANTEED INCOME

For Mark and Joanne to be truly happy, they need to enter retirement with their eyes wide open to the risks and dangers to their retirement. As mentioned in Chapter 1, to truly Master Your Retirement, you must be aware of these Seven Critical Risks so you can meet them head on and overcome them. The seven most critical risks to your long term lifestyle are: 1) inflation, 2) longevity, 3) investment returns, 4) market volatility, 5) timing of your retirement decision, 6) fees and 7) taxation. Let us now look at each briefly:

- **Inflation:** At an average inflation rate of 2%, the value of $1,000 twenty years from now will be only $667. This is a decline of 33% in the value of your income over 20 years of retirement. At an average rate of inflation of 3%, the decline is closer to 45%. Inflation is one of your greatest enemies to a long and comfortable retirement. Protecting against inflation will need to be a core component of your long term retirement income strategy.

- **Longevity:** As noted in the Introduction to this book, the average life expectancy today is approximately age 80 and rising. If you retire today at 55, you have a 50 − 50 chance of being retired for 25 or more years. Ironically, during your lifetime you have 25 to 30 years (beginning age 25 or 30 running to age 55) to live your life to the fullest, do everything you can for your kids, live in a nice home, drive a nice car and take nice vacations, all the while saving enough money to support your peak lifestyle at age 55 and pro-tecting that lifestyle against 25 to 30 years of inflation. When you think of it, this sounds quite unrealistic for most to accomplish.

The earlier you retire and the longer you live—your longevity—can be your greatest challenge, yet also your greatest goal. Alternatively, the longer you work, (no matter how small the capacity) the less longevity will be a factor.

- **Investment returns:** If your ideal investment returns are not achieved then your lifestyle may be at risk. The combination of conservative investment projections and small investment withdrawals are two ways you can ensure you meet your basic income needs.

- **Market volatility:** If you take on too much risk in your portfolio, you can be exposing your retirement vision to greater risks than you may be aware or be comfortable with. Most people are caught off guard when markets fluctuate. You need to understand and respect stock market fluctuations so as to ensure you are not a victim of this normal volatility.

- **Timing of your retirement date:** The timing of your retirement date is critical. The economy and the stock market do not care when your full pension date is realized or when you most wish to leave the work force. Given the length of the typical retirement period, the timing of your retirement date with the cycles of the economy is extremely important. Choosing this date is not a perfect science by any means, but making an informed decision will help you be better prepared for market fluctuations. Discuss this question with your advisors, the earlier the better. Even if you do not plan to retire for five – ten years, talk with your advisors now, they can assist you with future plans and strategies to combat the pressures of the economy.

- **Fees:** At the time you retire your portfolio may be the largest it will ever be. The fees you pay to have this portfolio managed throughout your retirement period may substantially impact your income, your risk profile and your estate value. For example, 66% of the portfolio management fees you pay during your lifetime will be charged during your retirement years. If you are choosing between two alternative investments, the one with the lower fees gives you the chance to take less risk to produce the same rate of return. Alternatively, should you achieve the same rate of return but, due to lower fees, keep more of your return each year, you may receive as much as 30% more total income throughout your retirement years and have as much as 47% more capital available to give to your heirs. These results are achieved with as little as a 1% difference in fees (e.g.: 1.5% management fees vs. 2.5%) over a 20 to 25 year period of time in retirement.

- **Taxation:** The tax you pay can also lead to a substantial decline in after-tax income. Tax efficiency in your portfolio and on your tax return is extremely important, as you will see in coming chapters. Tax inefficiency could lead to the clawback of tens of thousands of dollars of government benefits and unnecessary taxes paid over time.

THE TAX-EFFICIENT INCOME LAYERING PROCESS

With all of this being said, your focus is to create a tax-efficient, low risk income that will in turn give you considerable choices, freedom and peace of mind in retirement. We achieve this outcome through the income layering process.

Step #1: Identify Your Sources of Income

What are your sources of income?

- Government Benefits: Canada Pension Plan, Old Age Security, Guaranteed Income Supplement
- Private Pension Plans: Pension Plan, Individual Pension Plans
- Registered Savings: RRSPs, LIRAs
- Non-Registered Investments: Investment Accounts, Tax-Free Savings Accounts
- Home Equity
- Business/Farm
- Rental Property Income

Make a list of all of your different sources of income. Identify those sources which are guaranteed and those that will fluctuate.

Step #2: Understand What You Spend

To fully understand what you spend, consider the following steps:

Make a list of everything that you spend money on today. Divide the list into two groups: a) expenses that occur every month and b) expenses that typically occur once every year. By dividing the list into these two categories you can now see the timeline for your expenses.

Why is this important? If, for example, you need $2,000 available for taxes at the end of the year, you may find that you have not been able to save this money during the year. Instead, why not set aside a pool of money to pay these annual expenses when the time comes? This approach helps to align your expenses with certain investments and pools of capital.

Next, classify the monthly expenses into two categories: a) basic income needs and b) lifestyle income wants. Basic income needs are those expenses you incur today to support your basic needs such as the costs of living in your home (rent, mortgage, utilities, taxes, insurance), the costs of food and clothing, and basic expenses for transportation and entertainment. Lifestyle income wants include the upgrades to the life you prefer: a higher end cable package, living in an upscale neighborhood, driving an expensive car, golf or fitness club membership, season tickets for the arts or other sporting events, travelling at a higher standard and/or travelling more frequently, and so on.

Why is this important?

By breaking your monthly expenses into these two categories you begin to see the amount of income required to cover your basic needs as well as the amount of income required to cover your preferred lifestyle. Now you can begin to make some informed and important decisions. You begin to see how much money you really need to maintain your basic living needs. You also begin to see how much money goes towards those things that are nice to have, but not essential.

In most cases, people have enough (or more than enough) money to cover their basic income needs. Yet, many people may have just enough money (or not) to cover their lifestyle wants. An individual often becomes concerned about their finances and the fluctuation of either their income or their portfolio, when their lifestyle wants are at risk.

Due to the seven critical risks mentioned previously, the likelihood of having an ideal retirement outcome that will cover all of your lifestyle wants all of the time, may be, in reality, quite low. But, by breaking down your expenses in this way, you can begin to empower your financial resources to create the life you'd most like to live with as little risk as possible. This process helps to clarify precisely what is of value to you and what is not.

Are you better off trying to fund your current lifestyle with inadequate resources or are you better off adjusting your lifestyle to focus on those things that are most important to you within the boundaries of your available resources? It would be great to retire with more than enough money in which to live. However, with the volatility of the stock market and the fluctuations of the economy, you would need close to 20% more total assets just to buffer from these common occurrences. Now you not only need enough money to meet your peak lifestyle but 20% more.

Your retirement income plan must have flexibility and it must have a buffer. That is why it is so critically important to understand what you spend.

Step #3: Match Your Guaranteed Sources of Income with Your Basic Living Needs

Make a list of your guaranteed sources of income: for many these will be Canada Pension Plan benefits (age 60 or over), Old Age Security benefits (age 65 or over) and a Pension Plan benefit (from work). We can create additional guaranteed sources of income if necessary, but for now let's stick with the figures from the first three sources to begin our income and investment strategy.

When considering the Canada Pension Plan amount there are two specific items to address: a) timing (do you draw at age 60 or as late as age 65?) and b) ensuring that you have the maximum benefit amount available to you. In general you should take your Canada Pension Plan amount as early as possible (ideally age 60). In the event that you were out of the workforce for a number of years, due to being a stay at home parent, you can have these years removed from your Canada Pension Plan history which in turn creates a higher payment amount to you for the rest of your life. These options will be discussed in detail in Chapter 6.

Now that you have the figures for Canada Pension Plan, Old Age Security and your Pension Income, compare the total, after-tax monthly amount that you would receive with the basic monthly living expenses identified above. How close are these two numbers?

- Are your basic income needs covered by these guaranteed sources of income?
- How important is it to you to have your basic income needs covered by guaranteed sources of income?
- What percent of your total monthly income needs (basic needs + lifestyle needs) do you wish to have covered by guaranteed sources of income? 50%? 75%? 100%?

If your guaranteed income sources match or exceed your basic living needs, then you are on the right track. If not, then you may wish to consider converting some investment assets to an annuity so as to make sure all basic living needs are met through guaranteed income sources.

Step #4: Understand the Canadian Tax Structure to Get the Most from Your Friends in Government

As mentioned previously, it doesn't matter what you have, it only matters what you keep. The tax system, when used most efficiently, can make a substantial contribution to increasing your after-tax income.

As of the 2007 tax year, retired couples have the ability to split eligible pension income equally: Canada Pension Plan (in most cases), Old Age Security, Registered Pension Income (at age 60) and RRIF income (at age 65). Splitting income can be extremely beneficial because, in Canada we live in an increasing marginal rate of tax world. When your income crosses particular thresholds, every dollar you earn above that threshold is taxed at a higher rate. It is therefore important to split your incomes equally, as much as possible, to have two lower incomes rather than one large and one small income.

The Canadian tax system provides an age credit to those over age 65 earning less than $31,524 per year (in 2008). This credit will reduce your taxes. The credit can be as much as $5,276 (in 2008, indexed with inflation) per year, per spouse. Therefore, if you can have two incomes of $31,524 each you will pay the least amount of taxes and gain the highest level of credits. In Ontario in 2008 the age credit would contribute to providing a total after-tax monthly income of $4,662.32 (for the couple). Once you reach the $31,524 threshold this amount begins to be "reduced" at a rate of 15% per year.

To put this into context, $4,662.32 per month after-tax is the equivalent of one person earning an annual employment income of $73,500 (before tax). In this case the total tax paid would be $17,363.66. In the example of the 65 year old retired couple with the same after-tax income, their combined gross before tax income is only $63,048 (vs. $73,500) and the tax paid is only $7,100 (vs. $17,363.66). Income splitting and the tax credits have resulted in a $10,000 annual decrease in tax paid!

It is important to also keep in mind the Old Age Security clawback zone. Once you begin to earn an income of $64,718 (in 2008) or more your Old Age Security income begins to be taxed back at a rate of 15% per year. If your income is in this range, and you proceed to draw another $10,000 in RRIF income (using 2008 Ontario rate) you are paying the normal marginal tax rate plus the 15% clawback rate.

If you maximized the income between you and your spouse so that each of you were just under the clawback zone (and were age 65 or older), in Ontario your total monthly after-tax income would be approximately $8,342.62. Is this enough on which to live?

Why is this information important?

Understanding the tax system is extremely important because it helps to answer the question: "If I need more money than the basic guaranteed amounts noted above, which source of income do I draw from first?"

By understanding the tax system you can strategically draw the right amount of income from the right source at the right time. By doing so you can maximize the dollars received from the different levels of government while also maximizing your after-tax income.

To put these tax benefits into perspective, think about what you would need to do with your investment portfolio to create the same outcome. How much higher would your rate of return need to be to achieve the same after-tax income? How much more money would you need to have in your investment portfolio to·achieve the same after-tax income? By managing the taxes efficiently, you may be producing the equivalent benefit of increasing your rate of return from 5% to 9% or literally doubling the size of your portfolio. Managing the taxes allows you to focus on the future and not on the past; to focus on tax-efficient income rather than rate of return.

What if your income begins to creep into the OAS clawback zone?

This next section emphasizes the importance of strategically planning your retirement income years in advance. For example, what if you find that by age 65 your total income creeps into the OAS clawback zone? Remember, if this occurs you could also be creeping into a significant tax rate on any income earned above $65,000 per year.

To avoid the OAS clawback zone, you will need to have the flexibility to draw additional income from other sources that are not taxed at all or that are taxed at a reduced rate. Some tax-free sources of income can include: drawing equity from your principal residence, using mutual fund products that have a Tax Efficient Systematic Withdrawal Plan Feature (TSWP for short), a prescribed annuity and a Tax-Free Savings Account. The important point of the tax-free sources is the tax efficiency of the income received. You are able to receive the income you require while paying tax on a smaller amount of income, thereby avoiding the OAS clawback zone.

Why is the OAS clawback zone so important?

Old Age Security of approximately $500 per month is paid to virtually every Canadian at age 65 and older (note that there is a set of criteria that must be achieved). $1,000 per month for a couple aged 65, paid over 20 years is the equivalent to as much as $240,000 of additional income paid. This is significant.

Step #5: Prepare for the Future

It is important to look a few years down the road to ensure the decisions made today do not negatively impact your tax picture in the future. Plan ahead and do not put yourself in a situation whereby you are paying more taxes than necessary at any time in your life.

These five steps will help you become a Master of your income through all phases of retirement by layering your income in a tax-efficient manner.

THE 100% GUARANTEED SOLUTION

As mentioned previously, something is only as good as what you compare it to. Now that you have worked through the process of layering your retirement income, the question is whether you can create more income and more certainty. The purpose of this chapter is to create a high amount of after-tax income with as little risk as possible. This can be achieved by implementing, or at the very least, using the 100% Guaranteed Solution outlined below as a benchmark in which to compare other choices.

To create a guaranteed lifetime income you convert all of your assets to a lifetime pension plan structure called an annuity. If you annuitize all of your investments at the time you retire you will have a guaranteed income, for you and your spouse for life, regardless of how long either of you live.

If you wish to create a guaranteed benefit for your children as well, you should set up a joint last survivor life insurance plan. The proceeds of this insurance plan would be paid to your children upon the death of the last surviving spouse.

By purchasing the annuity, you would likely have more income than if you did not. This additional income would go towards financing the cost of the last survivor insurance. In many situations you would end up with 100% certainty as well as a higher annual income.

The 100% Guaranteed Solution is an important benchmark to measure all retirement income decisions against. The ideal scenario: a guaranteed lifetime income with no risk whatsoever. Any other option you set up for your retirement will require more risk. Therefore, you can always measure the size of potential benefit against the degree of additional risk. Is it really worth it to take on additional risks?

IN SUMMARY

THINGS YOU NEED TO KNOW

- Your odds for retirement success may depend more on "when" you retire as opposed to "how" you retire because of the impact that the economic cycle can have on your average portfolio returns.

- Understand the long term, after-fee rate of return for a balanced or conservative portfolio.

- If you have unrealistic expectations for return, it is possible you also have unrealistic expectations for risk, which can hurt you when financial markets fluctuate.

- Understand the seven critical risks to retirement and the challenge they can cause to your ideal retirement vision.

- Understand where your income fits into the Age Credit and Old Age Security clawback zones.

QUESTIONS YOU NEED TO ASK

- How much risk are you taking in your investment portfolio? What is the average annual compounded return over the past three, five and ten years? What is the worst one year return? How frequently is the bottom 20% of one year returns negative?

- Do your guaranteed sources of income match your basic living needs?

- How much income should come from guaranteed sources? How much income can be exposed to fluctuations in your portfolio?

- What is your marginal tax rate?

- Are you entering the Age Credit or Old Age Security clawback zones?

THINGS YOU NEED TO DO

- Work through the process of layering your income.
- Calculate the 100% guaranteed solution.
- Compare the results.
- Work with your advisor to develop your ideal portfolio.

DECISIONS YOU NEED TO MAKE

- Determine how much basic income you need.
- Determine the amount of additional lifestyle income required.
- Determine how much income is needed to cover monthly and any annual expenses.
- Determine the percent of income that is to come from guaranteed sources.

MASTER YOUR RETIREMENT
A Lifetime of Abundance, Choice, Low Risk and Guaranteed Income: A Dream Come True

TIPS

- The sum of money you have upon retirement is likely the largest it will ever be. The issue is how to get the most from your resources so you can achieve the retirement vision you desire.

- Think about how money can be a stress free component of retirement and not a stressor by considering options such as the 100% guaranteed solution.

- Plan ahead by taking into consideration the tax return and planning for tax-efficient income.

- Set up multiple sources of income where some is taxable and some is not.

- The timing of your retirement date may be the single most important factor when determining the level of success you will have in retirement. Be well-informed about economic conditions by discussing your planned retirement early and often with your advisors.

TRAPS

- Don't focus on the pre-tax rate of return. Focus only on after-tax income.

- Don't delay your planning. Forecast your income needs and your tax picture years in advance of age 65.

- Inflation, taxes and fees are three of the greatest risks to a long and healthy retirement; plan your retirement income with consideration on how these risks will affect you.

CHAPTER 3

Ten Critical Do's
and Don'ts of Retirement

The most splendid achievement of all is the constant striving to surpass your-self and to be worthy of your own approval. DENIS WAITLEY

> *Ron and Rachel Crumb are both age 57. They wish to decide how they should prepare for retirement, when they should retire and if they should retire.*
>
> *Ron owns and operates "The Crumby Bakery" that he founded 25 years ago. While he still enjoys the business he wishes to have more of a normal life with normal working hours. The bakery is quite successful with a staff of 10.*
>
> *Rachel is a lawyer at a local firm. She too is tired of the day to day grind and longs for days when she and Ron can spend their days together. They have always talked about spending more time trav-elling. They also want to spend more time at their condo in Florida. The kids are grown and on their own. Ron and Rachel have reasonable financial resources to retire and have zero debt.*
>
> *How should they prepare for retirement? What should they do and what should they avoid?*

THE ISSUES

In the first two chapters we talked about the importance of building a retirement vision and then vetting that vision through an understanding of portfolio risks, the seven critical retirement risks and the income layering process. The objective is to maximize monthly after-tax income while staying within important clawback zones on the tax return. We want to receive the highest reasonable amount of income, we want that income to be secure while paying the lowest amount of tax, and we want to have little to no risk of running out of money longer term.

Does this resonate with you? Do you have these same objectives?

Many retirees face the same questions as Rachel and Ron. Should they retire today or two years from now? Where should they live? What should they do with the business? How much income will they need? Will they have enough income? Will they run out of income? Where will this income come from? To answer these questions, Rachel and Ron need to build their vision for retirement. They need to think of their lives over the next 10 to 20 years. They need to imagine what their children (and grandchildren) will be doing during these same years and the extent to which they wish to be involved. They need to consider the top 100 things they wish to do as it relates to their health, activities and relationships.

When they do so, they may realize that they don't wish to spend all of their time in Florida. Ron may realize that he really wants to stay involved in the business. Rachel and Ron may also realize that taking the next three to five years at a slower pace is all they really need right now.

The important point to emphasize is that each may choose to retire in a different way. They are really planning two retirements and not just one. They also may choose to retire gradually and not all at once.

To bring together the concepts presented in the first two chapters, this chapter will focus specifically on the Ten Do's and Don'ts to consider as you contemplate retirement.

THE SOLUTIONS

DO Determine Your Canada Pension Plan Income Amount

In Chapter 2 we discussed the income layering process and the importance of identifying the guaranteed sources of income. The Canada Pension Plan (CPP) is one of the primary sources of income to serve this need.

To determine the amount of retirement income benefit you will receive, contact the local Service Canada office to get a printout of your projected CPP benefits. Assuming that both Ron and Rachel continue to work to age 60, they must take the "projected to age 65" amount and discount it by 30%. The full CPP benefit is available at age 65 assuming that you continue to make contributions up to that point in time. However, if you stop contributing to the Canada Pension Plan, or wish to begin to draw it earlier than age 65, then the amount you receive will be discounted. This discount is typically 6% of the full benefit amount per year. In this situation, if Rachel and Ron are both 60 and wish to retire and draw this income, the amount they will receive will be discounted by 6% for each year prior to 65 or 30% in total (5 years @ 6% per year = 30%).

To ensure that you receive the highest possible payment, check over the years of service to make sure the information provided is correct. If Rachel or Ron was out of the workforce (or worked fewer hours) for a number of years raising children, he or she can apply to have these years removed from his or her years of service. This is called the Child Rearing Provision. By reducing the number of years where there was no contribution to the plan, the retirement benefit received will be greater. This provision helps to increase the benefit amount received from CPP in retirement.

If Ron wishes to continue to work part time at the bakery, he could "retire" (show no income or less than the allowable maximum pension payment) for a period of two months (the month he applies and the 30 days following) and then begin to draw an income again from the business. He will then become eligible to receive his CPP benefit and stop paying CPP contributions. This is a significant step for all business owners to consider once they reach age 60.

Typically, it is recommended that you take your Canada Pension Plan benefit beginning age 60. If you were 65 today and planning to retire, the maximum benefit payment to you would be $885 per month (at the time of writing). If you were 60 today, and retiring, your benefit would be reduced by 30% of this amount. Your monthly retirement benefit would be approximately $619.50 per month. Should you take the lower amount at age 60 or the larger amount at age 65?

If all we did was add up the total amount received under each scenario, by age 76 the "CPP at age 65" amount would begin to exceed the total cumulative payments of the "CPP at age 60" alternative.

Alternatively, what if you were to retire at age 60, make no further contributions and not draw your CPP retirement benefit until age 65? Do the additional five years of "growth" increase your benefit?

If you retire at 60 and do not draw your CPP pension income until age 65, your maximum benefit will no longer be $885. Your benefit will be greater than $619.50 per month, but it will only reach the maximum benefit amount if you continue to contribute. Assuming that you do not contribute after age 60 your new breakeven point will be postponed by two to five more years.

Due to the uncertainty of life, it is best to take the CPP retirement income sooner rather than later.

DON'T Sell the Business

In most cases a business is worth much more as a long term going concern. Ron may find that the after-tax value of his business, if it were sold today, would produce nowhere near the income he could receive over time as a going concern.

To address this question, Ron will need to calculate the sale price of the business, estimate the taxes payable and then estimate the amount of after-tax income he could earn after the proceeds from the sale of the business were invested conservatively. How does this income compare with the income he receives today?

Ron has several options to consider.

- First, he could pull back from the day to day operations of the business, but maintain his role as owner by overseeing the operations.
- He could pay himself and Rachel dividends from the profits of the business each year, which could be a very tax effective source of income.
- Sell the business, but retain ownership in the land and building. If he were able to do so, he would continue to earn rental income as well as income from the invested proceeds of the sale of the business.

It is beneficial to explore each of these options so as to know the pros or cons of each alternative.

DO Enhance the Management Team of the Business

To give Ron the freedom to work a reduced workday and oversee the business from afar, he must spend time grooming a senior manager. The business must not be dependent on Ron, his contacts or his abilities. If the business was dependent on Ron being in the building each and every day, the business is truly worth much less than Ron would believe. A business has the greatest value when it is not dependent on the skills or contacts of the owner. Ron's number one objective is to make himself redundant. He needs to groom others to do what he is doing today and to encourage them to do those tasks even better than he does.

DON'T Sell Your Home

The first two years of retirement will often involve significant levels of change and adjustment. What you may have thought retirement would be like may prove to be completely different. Your home is one of your most important retirement assets. The proceeds from the sale of your home, as your principal residence under the Income Tax Act, are completely tax-free.

Since the equity in your home is "tax-free", if you were to set up an equity line of credit you could gradually draw on this line of credit as you needed additional income. This money would be tax-free to you. The downside to this approach is the fact that you would now have to make interest payments on the borrowed money.

To avoid the interest payment situation, a "reverse mortgage" is another option to consider. In this scenario you are tapping into a portion of the tax-free equity in your home. As you draw on this equity, you are being charged interest at a rate that is typically higher than the interest rate you are charged as a straight home equity line of credit. You need to make sure you are fully aware of the interest costs and the implications of these higher interest costs over time. However, the benefit is that you do not have to make regular interest payments on the money drawn. The bad news is that at some point in time you do have to pay the interest. The interest is typically paid when the home is sold. This may mean that when the home is sold you have little to no equity left. In other words, the value of the home may be needed to pay off the reverse mortgage. A reverse mortgage is a good option to consider, but you need to be very careful how and when you tap into it due to the longer term consequences of the compounding interest cost.

DO Consider the 100% Guaranteed Approach

The "ideal" retirement plan is more easily determined if you can compare it to a fully guaranteed retirement scenario such as the 100% Guaranteed Approach discussed in Chapter 2.

For example, if at age 60 Ron and Rachel decided to convert all of their RRSPs and non-registered investments to a lifetime pension they will be able to see exactly how much income they would receive over their lifetime. This income is guaranteed for life.

To determine this amount, project forward the value of the investments to age 60. Then, with the assistance of a "life insurance licensed advisor" prepare a "lifetime annuity" quote beginning at age 60 and running for life. Consider an annuity quote that contains the following details: the income is guaranteed for a minimum of 15 years and the quote is based on 100% to the last survivor. This will give you the most conservative lifetime annuity income. You should consider quotes from multiple firms as this is a competitive area and different firms will offer different payment amounts.

The 100% guaranteed solution includes a joint last survivor life insurance policy, that will provide a lump sum tax-free payment to your beneficiaries. How much should this lump sum payment be? It can either be an amount that you have chosen to give to your children, or it can be the projected after-tax value of your current investments. As a rule of thumb consider 50% of the value of your current RRSP investments + 75% of your current non-registered investments. When calculating the payment amount we recommend you consider the "contractually guaranteed minimum interest rate" in the policy as your projected rate of return. For many contracts today this would be in the 2% to 3% range. By doing so your insurance premium payment may be greater than what you may wish to pay but it creates a guaranteed payment amount that is unlikely to change in the future.

Now calculate the after-tax value of your annuity income (plus your other sources of income) and subtract the cost of the life insurance. This solution is now a 100% guaranteed solution. The income is guaranteed for life no matter what happens and the kids are guaranteed to receive a fixed amount of after-tax money. More importantly, all alternative retirement scenarios can be compared to this guaranteed solution. Any other alternative scenario will be of greater risk than this scenario. The question is: how much risk do you have to take to achieve a higher income, and will it be worth it?

Ron and Rachel now have a firm benchmark for a fully guaranteed retirement. They can now use this information to decide the pros and cons of annuitizing some of their assets and not others. They can compare this information with their basic income needs and their enhanced lifestyle wants. Ron and Rachel may also decide to implement this strategy three, five or even ten years from now.

DON'T Move to Florida

Don't rush into moving to another city, province or country right away. Many couples find that while they may prefer the more moderate climate of another city or country, they miss the connection with family and friends back home. For many couples the loneliness that sometimes occurs when living away from their historical home base may drive them to return just a few short years after moving.

It is also important to understand that by moving to the U.S. you may be faced with other issues such as the real or "deemed disposition" of Canadian property. As a result you may be facing a significant tax bill, even though you did not physically sell the assets.

By moving to the U.S. you may also lose your access to Canadian health care benefits while potentially gaining exposure to U.S. estate taxes.

Owning property in the U.S. has pros and cons. If you rent the property to others you may be facing addition U.S. income tax as well as U.S. estate taxes when you die.

Owning property or permanently moving to the U.S. is a complicated situation and should be well researched before making the final decision. You should seek the advice of an expert in this area. Many of the national accounting firms have specific expertise in this area.

DO Review Your Sources of Health Care Benefits

Should Ron and Rachel retire? One of the factors to consider is the health care benefits they receive from their current employment. If Ron continues to work in his business he could maintain family benefits under his group plan for several more years. Ron and Rachel should research the cost of private health care plans. The difference in cost may encourage one or both of them to continue to work part time for several more years. Close to 70% of your total lifetime health expenditures occur in the last few years of life and can become a significant monthly expense.

DON'T Postpone Activities

Many people will postpone activities until they retire. They say they will join a health club once they retire or they will eat better when they have the time to plan their meals. In most cases these new activities will only happen if you are successful in making them new habits. Those who are able to truly master their retirement will begin those activities now so they are entrenched when they officially retire. Doing so will help to make the transition to retirement seamless and gradual. A wholesale change in the way you spend your days is not something that begins overnight just because you are retired. Don't postpone important activities. Try them out now and create new habits today. Try them out now to see if you like them and to see if they "stick". Retirement doesn't have to be an all or nothing event. Rather, it could be a series of gradual transitions, new activities and new habits spread out over five to ten years of time.

DO Consider Alternative Retirement Scenarios in Your Planning Process

There are many different ways Ron and Rachel can approach their retirement years. They could both retire at the same time or at different times. They could gradually reduce their work over the next several years and begin retiring over time. One spouse could retire outright while the other retires gradually.

From a financial point of view, consider the 100% guaranteed solution and measure it against all other possible income solutions that may have little to no guarantees.

Professional financial advice can be obtained from many varied sources. Think of your advisors as a team who are helping you develop a winning game plan. Your most trusted advisor on this team becomes the "quarterback" delivering the right solutions for your retirement vision. However, be careful with this process as some concepts can be presented that may sound very appealing, yet contain certain degrees of risk, expenses are based on unrealistic assumptions. Always keep in mind the seven critical risk factors mentioned in Chapter 2.

In general, Ron and Rachel may wish to consider one or more of the following:

- **100% Guaranteed Solution:** This would include selling the business outright and buying an annuity with the process.

- **100% Interest Only Solution:** Sell the business outright and invest the proceeds conservatively. In this scenario you would calculate the interest income (assume 4% or 5%) of the capital you have available to invest.

- **Keep the Business Solution:** Ron continues to receive income from the business in the form of either salary or dividends. Additional income is drawn from other resources as required to meet the after-tax income objective.

- **Retire to the U.S. Solution:** Pay all taxes when departing Canada and the net proceeds invested for income (using either the 100% Guaranteed Solution or the 100% Interest Only Solution above).

- **Tax-efficient Income Solution:** This approach is exactly the opposite of the Interest Only Solution mentioned above. In this scenario, Ron and Rachel identify the amount of after-tax income needed to meet their objectives. The first source of income would be CPP, the next source of income would be from investments and the third source of income would be from the business. By following this approach they will be able to determine the amount of income that needs to come from the business as well as the form in which it should be drawn (i.e.: as a salary or as a dividend). This approach follows the income layering steps discussed in Chapter 2.

In each of these approaches, you may consider retiring at 60, 63 or 65. You can use one or a combination of these strategies. By preparing these alternative plans, you are able to see the future impact of the decisions you make today. This will ensure the decisions you make today do not unlock any unintended consequences or surprises.

DON'T Draw all of Your Income from Variable Sources

If all, or the vast majority, of your income is to come from your actively managed investment portfolio consider the following risks.

A negative return in any one year will decrease your capital value. If this occurs over the first 12 to 24 month period of retirement you may never regain the previous portfolio value. This money may be lost forever.

The probability of running out of money heightens when you retire at the tail end of a bull market. Remember, the stock market and economy move in cycles that range from periods of growth to periods of recession. This is the natural flow of our economy. Due to this flow, the stock market will also ebb and flow from periods of growth to periods of decline. We refer to the periods of growth as a bull market and the periods of decline as a bear market.

If you were to retire towards the end of a bull market, the stock market may see considerable declines. If this were the case, as mentioned in the previous section, your probability of running out of money is greatly enhanced. Alternatively, if you retire at the beginning of the next bull market (perhaps just two or three years later) you are more likely to pass away with more money than what you started with in retirement. Timing is everything.

Considering all these factors, it is best to think in terms of a range of retirement dates and how they relate to the economy and the business cycle, rather than picking one "ideal" retirement date. Remember, the economy and the business cycle have no interest or concern as to your preferred retirement date. Yet, we know from history that if you pay attention to, and respect these cycles, you may save yourself from a great deal of pain.

In the first two years of retirement, it is valuable to set aside one or two years of income inside a high interest savings account for easy access. This will help to buffer your portfolio should the market decline within the first few years of retirement.

IN SUMMARY

THINGS YOU NEED TO KNOW

- There are many different ways to structure your retirement income plan.
- There are considerable tax implications in moving or owning property in the U.S.
- 70% of your total lifetime health care costs occur in the last 10 years of your life. Planning to have lower cost health care benefits available to you should be an important part of your planning process.
- In most situations you will want to take your CPP retirement income benefit at as early an age as possible.
- Entrepreneurs should speak with their accountant to structure the best way to begin drawing the CPP benefit at age 60 and stop making contributions.

QUESTIONS YOU NEED TO ASK

- Am I scheduled to receive the right amount of CPP retirement income benefits?
- Can my spouse or I qualify for the Child Rearing Provision and thus increase the retirement income benefits paid?
- Is my business more valuable to me as an ongoing entity or is it more valuable to me if I sell it outright?
- Can I train others to run my business on a day to day basis?
- If I set up a reverse mortgage, what are the long term implications if I live a long and fruitful life? Will I be able to access additional home equity, or will it all be tied up in the reverse mortgage?
- What are the fees and tax implications of each decision?
- When compared to the 100% Guaranteed Solution, what other scenarios give me more income within a smaller degree of risk?

THINGS YOU NEED TO DO

- Prepare your retirement vision.
- Review your CPP benefit amounts.
- If necessary, find someone who can help you quantify the pros and cons of different options that relate to the business.
- If necessary, find someone who can help you quantify the pros and cons of moving to Florida.
- Begin to create different retirement income models that focus on the bottom line, after-tax income received.
- Do some research and ask the opinions of others as to where we are in the current market cycle.

DECISIONS YOU NEED TO MAKE

- Should we move?
- Should we sell the business?
- Decide to retire gradually or all at once?
- When should I begin drawing my Canada Pension Plan benefits?
- How can I (we) draw the income needed, in the most tax-efficient manner?
- If I set up a reverse mortgage, will I be able to access additional home equity or will it all be tied up in the reverse mortgage?
- Do I have an advisory team that can help me with my retirement planning?

MASTER YOUR RETIREMENT
10 Critical Do's and Don'ts
for Retirement

TIPS

- Go through this chapter again and make a note of the 10 Do's and Don'ts. Identify the ones that are most applicable to you and then rank them in order of importance.
- Ask your advisors how they approach retirement income planning and compare what they say with the ideas mentioned throughout this book. Spend time interviewing three to five advisors to compare how they approach retirement income planning.
- Ask your advisor to show you the after-tax monthly income amounts.
- Speak to other retired people about health care insurance plans to gain feedback on the best alternatives to consider in your region.

TRAPS

- The retirement planning process can be complex, give it the time it needs—don't rush it.
- It is easy to become bogged down in the details when you are doing your planning. When this happens, set it aside for a few weeks and then come back to it.

CHAPTER 4

Living the Life
You'd Love to Brag About

When patterns are broken, new worlds emerge. TULI KUPFERBERG

Terry and Trish have been retired for five years. They have done most of the things they set out to do in retirement. They have taken a couple of trips, got together with some long lost friends, spent time helping out their kids and grandkids and spent more time golfing and playing tennis. Terry and Trish are both in their late 60s and have seven beautiful grandchildren. Two of their children live in other provinces so they travel a couple of times a year to see them. Terry and Trish have been living their ideal retirement vision. But now, after just five short years some cracks are beginning to appear.

They are concerned that they are getting into a rut. They are not unhappy with their current life; it just seems that they have been living the same year of life over and over again. It appears that this will continue for the foreseeable future unless they do something about it.

Even though they have been active up to now, it has become easier and easier to stay home due to fatigue and frankly, a lack of urgency. Since it is very easy to put off to tomorrow what could have been done today, Terry and Trish have both recognized they aren't as motivated to stay as active as they used to be. For the first time in many years they are both putting on weight. Is it time for a change? Should they think about getting involved in something different?

As they have become less active they are spending more time doing things on their own, rather than together. Over the past few months they have had more confrontations and conflicts than usual. They have also found that they are spending less time social-izing with their friends. Their friends have all evolved and changed and they are finding that they just don't enjoy the time together with friends as much as they used to. Perhaps, it is time to think about meeting some new people? Yet, who wants to do so at this time in their life?

They want to "live the life they'd love to brag about", but are unsure of where to turn. They are looking for things they can be excited about. After five good years, where do they go from here?

THE ISSUES

Terry and Trish have done the things they thought they'd always do in retirement, yet are left wanting more. They are in a rut that may begin to cause a rift in their relationship. They are becoming less active. They are becoming less social. They are becoming less stimulated and excited about their life. They are faced with a difficult, yet very common, question: will we continue to live the same year of life over and over again, or will we break the routine and try something different. Will they live one year of retirement 20 times over a 20 year period of retirement or will they continue to grow as people in an interesting and engaging manner?

Think about the following questions:

- Did your marriage last this long just because you are a really great companion…or did you have to work at it?

- Could you count on your next job promotion just because you showed up at work on time each day...or did you have to push yourself to go for more training or education?
- Do you have relationships with many different people just because you are someone that everyone else wants to be around...or did you have to work at maintaining those relationships?
- Do you have a great relationship with your kids and grandkids just because everyone loves to be with you...or did you have to make some sacrifices and make an extra effort for these relationships to grow and thrive?
- Are you fit and in good physical shape at this stage in your life because of your diet of coffee and pizza...or have you had to work hard on both your diet and your exercise?

You most certainly have had to work hard to obtain whatever was important to you in your life: the relationship with your spouse and children, your career advancements, relationships with friends and your health. Just because you are now retired, does this mean that you can coast for the next 20 years or does this mean that you may have to continue to work hard at a few things from time to time? Perhaps this will be even more difficult for you during this time due to your aging body? Perhaps you will have to work even harder for these things than you have had to in the past?

THE SOLUTIONS

In Chapter 1 we talked about the importance of creating a vision for your retirement. In Chapter 2 we talked about how to deal with many of the financial aspects related to retirement. In Chapter 3 we discussed the 10 most important decisions to consider. These are all big picture planning issues and considerations.

Now we will spend more time dealing with the day to day realities of retirement. We want you to truly "live the life you'd love to brag about".

To achieve this dream, three things need to happen:

- **Focus on possibilities:** Focus on doing the little things well on a day to day basis. In the context of retirement planning, it is important to be acutely aware of the issues that need to be resolved, the things that need to be fixed, and the things you'd love to do, learn or improve.

- **Your purpose needs to be bigger than you:** Think in terms of your lasting legacy. A legacy is many things. It is your contribution to meaningful activities, it is the joy, memories and ideas that are left with others for years to come and it is also your financial contributions. Having a clearly defined legacy, for many people, is a very motivating, energizing and empowering aspect of their life.

- **Your relationships need to grow and evolve:** As time goes on and family roles change, relationships will change as well. Your relationship with others will change as their roles are evolving— a daughter becomes a mother, a son becomes a father.

These three steps are not exclusive to just retirement planning, but in planning for a healthy, happy and productive life.

FOCUS ON THE POSSIBILITIES

One of the ways for Terry and Trish to get out of the rut they are in today is to focus on a wide range of new possibilities. It will be these possibilities that will give them increased motivation, passion and energy in their day to day lives.

For example, in most people's lives, regardless of their stage in life, there are things to:

- Resolve.
- Fix.
- Do.
- Learn.
- Improve.

As a matter of fact, you can make this into a game where the purpose of the game is:

- To push your personal boundaries.
- To support your spouse in how they wish to push their own personal boundaries.

Create a "Jar of Possibilities" that is filled with pieces of paper where each piece of paper contains a possibility. On each piece of paper is an item to Resolve, Fix, Do, Learn or Improve. It is something that the husband could add to on his own, or his spouse could add to on his behalf, and vice versa.

For example:

- **Things to resolve:** These are the unsolved problems with the important people in your life. Perhaps it is a broken relationship that needs mending, a conflict that should be addressed or a miscommunication that needs time for discussion. Address these issues today and over time you will be happier, healthier and more active. These unresolved issues can drain your energy and can cause to you become demoralized and isolated from family and friends. Resolving these unresolved issues will be like lifting a huge weight off your shoulders.
- **Things to fix:** Perhaps these are physical jobs around the house, or perhaps these are established and somewhat negative personality traits that you would like to change. As with most other things in life, when these issues remain unresolved, they can be a burden. Now that you are retired you have the time and ability to explore those things you'd love to fix.
- **Things to do:** Have you seen some of the museums or art galleries that are located in your area? Would you like to become more involved with local charities? Would you like to be more involved in coaching, teaching or certain sporting activities? What would you love to challenge your spouse to do in this area? Have you always wanted to write down the stories of your childhood or teach others how to paint?

- **Things to learn:** Keeping your mind active and challenged is extremely important in retirement. A healthy, active and vibrant mind can often translate into a healthy, active, and vibrant lifestyle. What is it that you always wanted to learn? Have you wanted to learn more about your family history, how to be a gourmet cook or play a musical instrument? Have you wanted to learn more about politics, gardening, woodworking or finance? Now is the time. A few hours a week and you can meet new people with similar interests.

- **Things to improve:** What would you love to do better? What would you like to challenge your spouse to do better? Would you like to improve your fitness, golf game, relationships with your grandchildren?

Challenge yourself to do more than just what may come naturally and you will "live the life you'd love to brag about". Without a plan, you may find that you are doing plenty of things, but none which are really challenging you in any way. What are the limits of your comfort zone and what do you need to do to push that comfort zone? This is what living a full and abundant life is all about.

THE JAR OF POSSIBILITIES GAME IN ACTION

Every Monday morning Terry and Trish set aside time to discuss specific topics under one of several important categories (resolve, fix, do, learn or improve).

For example, under the topic of resolving something, Terry and Trish have learned that the key to a boisterous retirement is to remove the obstacles to happiness. In Terry's case this meant resolving a troubled relationship that he had with his brother. Terry and Trish talked about what this issue meant to Terry and how it could be resolved. They developed a game plan and Trish has supported Terry every step along the way to help with this healing process. Today, Terry and his brother get together for a game of golf every couple of weeks. While their relationship is still a little tense at times, they are spending more time together than they ever have. This has been very energizing for Terry.

In another discussion, Trish needed to fix something—her lifetime habit of controlling the kids. While she was a natural and was very good at it, she soon realized that she needed to let go and change this behaviour. By developing a game plan, Trish has been able to reduce the level of stress in her life, and her children's life, considerably. This has relieved the tension when the children visit and they have been dropping over more often.

One day Trish and Terry explored the topic of "doing something". They both wanted to give back and do something more for those less fortunate in their community. They had never had much time to volunteer when they were working and raising their family and it was very much outside of their comfort zone. However, they talked about this with other friends and found two other couples who volunteer weekly at a local soup kitchen. Now they do this together as a social outing that is enjoyable and helps them feel good about giving back to their community.

On another occasion Trish and Terry wrote down a number of different ideas that they thought would be fun to challenge the other person to "learn something new". They each wrote down 10 different ideas and put them into two different jars, one for Terry and one for Trish. The jars remain in the kitchen and are added to regularly throughout the month. At the beginning of each month they draw one piece of paper from their respective jar. During the month the challenge is to complete the task of learning the suggestion on the paper. In one instance Trish challenged Terry to get familiar with using e-mail. In another situation Terry challenged Trish to learn more about pairing wines with certain meals. A month later Trish challenged Terry to learn to barbecue three new fish dishes. In that same month Terry challenged Trish to spend more time learning how to paint, something that she has always wanted to do.

When the time came to discuss improvements, the conversation gravitated toward diet, health and exercise. Each has supported the other in setting and attaining small monthly goals related to their health, exercise, activity level and weight.

Terry and Trish have kept track of all of the things they have accomplished together since they began the Jar of Possibilities game. They also keep a list of all of the things they wish to discuss sometime in the future. This has been a fun, enlightening and empowering experience for both. They are energetic and active, both mentally and physically. This has lead to greater feelings of happiness and satisfaction and has also brought them closer together as a couple. They are a stronger team today than they have ever been.

Terry and Trish are "living the life they love to brag about" because they are constantly learning, improving their health, resolving outstanding issues, and spending time with the people they love. They know that their life today has no boundaries. They also know that they will always support each other in everything they do. They have overcome obstacles. They have examined their own fears and they have improved themselves.

Terry and Trish are mastering their life together. They have the time, freedom and flexibility to do so. As a matter of fact, they have also begun to share their knowledge and enthusiasm with others through a website that they have built together.

For Terry and Trish, "living the life they love to brag about" is not necessarily about spending more money, but evaluating how they spend their time.

Is this example realistic or is it just fantasy? Do you believe that once you have reached retirement that the relationship you have with your spouse is probably already entrenched and is not likely to change? Do you feel your spouse is capable of changing? Do you feel you or your spouse could benefit from dealing with some unresolved issues? Perhaps in a mischievous way, what would you love to challenge your spouse to do, to resolve, to learn about or to fix? How would you answer the same questions for yourself?

The Jar of Possibilities game is all about challenging yourself on a day to day basis. These challenges are meant to give you ideas, energy and optimism every day of your life.

YOUR PURPOSE NEEDS TO BE BIGGER THAN YOU

At the end of the day, what will be your legacy? It may give you a great sense of purpose and passion throughout your retirement and may take you to places you have never dreamed and it may introduce you to people that inspire you to achieve more.

A legacy may come in several different forms. It may be your contributions to an organization or cause. It may be the memories of joy and laughter with your children and grandchildren. It may be things that you write down and share with generations to come. Your legacy may also be a financial contribution. Regardless of what you choose, your legacy can give you a great sense of passion and purpose and contribute to an abundant and full life.

When you are considering your legacy, ask yourself these questions:

- When the retirement party is over, what type of legacy will you have from your work? For most people, despite the enjoyment experienced during their working years, after retirement, their contributions are often soon forgotten. Does your "life's work" need to be something more than just a life filled with work?

- Can money truly buy you happiness?

- What are the greatest memories you have of your life? Are they the times when you played it safe, or when you made more money? Were they the times when you were with friends and family? Or perhaps they were the times when you went out of your comfort zone and lived to tell about it!

- In some cases, retired couples will begin to feel disillusioned early on in retirement. It is common for people to ask the question "Is this all there is to life?" Now that you've reached retirement, are you now just waiting to get sick and die?

Some people decide to take significant, yet well planned and calculated risks so as to really change the status quo. For some it may be travelling abroad for the first time. For some it may be volunteering in a soup kitchen or delivering Meals on Wheels. For some it may be writing their memoirs. For some it may be learning a new activity or sport. For some it may be starting a home based business.

Remember, retirement is a truly unique time in life when you have a foundation income (that is non-work related). This foundation gives you choices and flexibility with how you spend your time. The greatest risk to a full retirement, and "living the life you'd love to brag about", is staying within your comfort zone.

> *With these questions in mind, Terry and Trish began to think more about their legacy and as a result began to explore the possibility of international humanitarian work. They researched the different possibilities and found that they could spend as much as two years away providing educational training and other assistance to people in impoverished nations. Terry and Trish decided to sell their home and structure their investments very conservatively.*

> *After this experience Terry and Trish had a tremendous legacy of friendships, experiences and accomplishments that will benefit generations to come. They also documented their experiences in a book and, using an on-line book publishing service, produced copies for all family members. In the book are the stories of an incredible seven years living abroad and the lessons learned that Terry and Trish wished to pass on to their own grandchildren. Terry now volunteers to speak about their experiences to church groups and university classes throughout the year.*

Perhaps your lasting legacy consists of:

- Volunteering your time as a Boy Scout leader.
- Working with children at a local school: Contact the school and offer to spend time over the lunch hour teaching a small group of kids about a topic you have an interest or skill in, such as wood-working, sporting activities, public speaking, nutrition, finances.
- Volunteering at a before school program serving breakfast to make sure kids are fed in the morning and ready to learn.
- Hosting exchange students from another country: This gives you the chance to meet young people from around the world.

These activities are examples of things you can do, from time to time throughout the year, that contribute to building your lasting legacy of memories, joy and wisdom.

Your legacy consists of the things you have done to enhance the world around you. This can be done through your actions as well as through your finances. You may find that your legacy projects give you great passion, meaning and inspiration.

YOUR RELATIONSHIPS NEED TO GROW AND EVOLVE

As you move into retirement and perhaps grandparent mode, your role within the family has changed. In some instances, these changes may create conflict. You need to be aware of the possibility of conflict.

For most people, family is everything. There is no greater joy than to see your children graduate from school, find a great spouse, marry and start a family. It is truly a miraculous, joyful and abundant time of life. Yet, one of the challenges during this time is to learn how to be a fabulous grandparent.

It is natural to want to provide wisdom, experience, support and encouragement to your children during this time. Yet, your children may not always be appreciative of your efforts or in agreement with your wisdom. You know from experience that over time your children have eventually appreciated your concerns, ideas and input, but you also know in most situations they have to learn life's lessons on their own.

In many situations grandparents are as emotionally attached to the grandchildren as are the parents. For the grandparent, the challenge is to know when to be there for support and when to step back and wait to be asked.

Many families cannot help but get into very deep and divided encounters when it comes to the grandchildren. Some times the grandparents, when the grandchildren are under their watchful eye, can not help but contradict some of the values or beliefs of the parents. A strong and vocal grandparent, who has always been in a leadership role both in the family and in the outside world, cannot help but be a very vocal and opinionated grandparent. This may be the life long pattern of the relationship between what is now the grandparent and the parent and a pattern that probably needs to be broken if the relationships are to survive and grow.

The key to improving these relationships in setting boundaries.

Physical Boundaries

- Separate residences are the ideal for grandparents and grandchildren. This gives the grandparents an opportunity to go home and "get a break" from the grandkids. It also creates the opportunity for the grandchildren to have a "sleepover" at the grandparent's house. Some of our greatest memories growing up have been the "one on one" time with our grandparents.

- By having this physical boundary it is easier for the parents to give in a little on the parenting issues. After all, what happens at grandma and grandpa's home is their business. However, the "behaviour expectations" at the child's home stand. This type of consistency and clarity is extremely important for the child to learn about boundaries. In some situations, it can be the opposite and the behaviour expectations are much greater when the children visit grandma and grandpa than when they are at home. It is substantially easier for the grandparent to be a grandparent when they are not physically living in the same premises. This physical boundary clearly distinguishes the role of the parents as the disciplinarians and the role of the grandparent as, well, the grandparent.

The Activity Related Boundaries

It is easy for the grandparent to do the laundry, clean the house, do the grocery shopping and prepare the meals while he/she is also looking after the grandchild. After all, the parents are away at work, weaving their way through the challenges and stresses of the day. Isn't this the least they could do to "help out"? Isn't this just being "nice"?

Absolutely, it is a very nice thing to do...from time to time. For some couples they may find that they are losing control of their own life when all of these things are being done for them. However, on occasion, as a surprise, the gesture is greatly appreciated.

Is the grandparent expected to discipline the grandchild? This may be something that the grandparent naturally gravitates to so as to maintain their own sanity. However, this may be in conflict with the values or approaches preferred by the parents. Naturally, there will be different views on parenting simply because the grandparents and the parents are from different generations. Also, since each of the parents was raised in a different manner, there is always a natural conflict that occurs between parents on what is right and wrong. It may take weeks, months or years for the parents to see eye to eye on certain parenting approaches. The grandparents' contribution to this may create greater confusion for the grandchild and frankly, may create additional conflict in the relationship between the parents.

Time is also an important boundary. If the grandchild spends more time with the grandparent than with the parent, it is natural for the child to see the grandparent as the "go to person" on most issues. This may deeply sadden the parents over time as they may find that they are missing out on the challenges, joys and frustrations of being a parent. This may create resentment and conflict between the children, the parents and the grandparents.

IN SUMMARY

No two retirements are alike. Even the questions surrounding one's retirement can be very different, even though the objectives are the same. To "do" retirement is one thing. To truly Master Your Retirement by "living the life you'd love to brag about" is something very different.

We want to challenge you to "take more risks", "take initiative", and "take action" on the things that you may not have considered before. If the goal is to "live the type of life you'd love to brag about" then perhaps this should be seen as your inspirational call to action. To truly Master Your Retirement is to challenge yourself, your spouse and the status quo; it is to build your lasting legacy of memories, joy and wisdom; and it is to enhance your relationships to a deeper level.

If these things are not in place, you will likely have some frustrations and challenges throughout your retirement.

THINGS YOU NEED TO KNOW

- It is very easy to get in a rut after just two or three years of retirement.
- It is easy to lose your energy and your focus when your goals and purpose are not clear.
- The Jar of Possibilities is a great way to keep things lively and interesting, both personally, and within your marriage/partnership relationship.
- A clearly defined lasting legacy is an amazing motivator and energizer. A lasting legacy can be many things including your contribution to a meaningful cause, the sharing of insight and wisdom, writing down the family stories, sharing laughter and fun with family and friends as well as lasting financial gifts.
- Relationships with your children and grandchildren will change and evolve over the years. It is important to recognize how you should adapt to these changes so that your relationships will continue to grow.

QUESTIONS YOU NEED TO ASK

- Am I in a rut today? Do I need to try something new or shake things up? Is the same true for my spouse?
- If you could challenge your spouse to do one thing, what would that be?
- If you could take one risk over the next 12 months, what would you do?
- What do you want to be known for? How do you want others to remember you?
- Are you living out the vision you have of your lasting legacy?
- If you could do one thing over the next 12 months to enhance your lasting legacy, what would you do?
- Are you concerned about one or more specific relationships with your children or grandchildren? What do you feel you need to do to enhance that relationship?

THINGS YOU NEED TO DO

- Find a jar. Label it "Jar of Possibilities". Cut up pieces up paper, put ideas on the paper, and put the paper beside the jar. Put the jar in a prominent location in your home so that you will see it throughout each day.
- Every Monday morning sit down and draw one item from the jar. Focus on that one item over the next one to two weeks.
- Think about those people (past or present) whom you really admire. What is it that you admire about them?
- Think about a cause or a mission that is bigger than you are. Talk about this with your spouse and friends. What is it? Perhaps this is something that you can do together with others.
- Read books about grandparenting.
- Be supportive of your children and keep the dialogue open.

DECISIONS YOU NEED TO MAKE

- How can I be a better parent? Grandparent?
- What will be my lasting legacy?
- What would I like to learn?
- What can I improve?

MASTER YOUR RETIREMENT
Living the Life
You'd Love to Brag About

TIPS

- Be honest with yourself. Are you truly happy? Are you feeling run down? Are you feeling unfulfilled? If so, have the courage to take action.

- At exactly the point when things are going well, change them up. Challenge the status quo so that you don't fall into another rut.

- Seek out new friendships or groups in which to associate.

- Make your health a top priority. The more time you have to execute your "vision" the greater the outcome will be.

TRAPS

- Don't let your "self-concept" hold you back. Many people will look in the mirror, or at their age, and then automatically count themselves out of being able to do certain things. Great joy comes from trying something new and succeeding. Don't let your "self-concept" hold you back.

- Don't assume that your "legacy" is something that is only "financial". Your legacy can mean many different things.

- Don't assume that a "financial legacy" is something that only "rich people" can do. Even small amounts of money can make a huge difference over time.

- Don't assume that your relationships with your children will always be the same. They will change and evolve as everything else does in this world.

CHAPTER 5

Your Home is Your Castle, and Don't Forget It!

When you were born, you cried and the world rejoiced. Live your life so that when you die, the world cries and you rejoice. CHEROKEE EXPRESSION

Sam and Jennifer Smart are both age 63. Sam is retiring from a job with the federal government and Jennifer is retiring from a career in teaching. They both have excellent pensions, $300,000 in additional investments and are debt free. They have a second home in Florida and a cottage about two hours away.

The kids are grown and on their own. The first grandchild arrived a year ago and they expect to see many more over the next 10 years.

At this stage they are wondering if it is time to downsize their home. They expect to be living at the cottage most of the summer and spending more time at their Florida home each winter. While spending half the year at the cottage is appealing, they worry that they may miss the contact with family and friends back in the city. Do they really want the cottage or could they use this money for something else?

Just up the road is a new 55+ condominium development under construction. Getting in at this stage would give them the chance to add some custom features that are important to them. Yet, when all is said and done they will have a smaller home, they will no longer have green space around them, and they will end up with a mid-sized mortgage.

What should they do? Should they jump at this chance to move into a nice new condo complex?

What should they do about the cottage? Should they sell it and use the proceeds for the new condo or should they assume that the kids will wish to use the cottage in the future?

Even though they like to be in Florida during the winter, they also know that they would like to travel more. Should they keep the Florida home, should they sell it and use the proceeds elsewhere or should they rent it and make some money from the property?

THE ISSUES

There are several issues facing Sam and Jennifer.

First of all, they have considerable money tied up in real estate that they use for short periods of time each year. This money could be used to finance other real estate purchases or to fund lifestyle choices. It could also be used to assist their children in buying their first homes.

They are also unsure of what to do with each of their properties. How much will they use each property from this point forward? As they age, will they be able to use and enjoy each property? Does it make sense to buy the new condo and commit to a mortgage at this stage in their lives?

What is the state of the current real estate market? Is this the right time to be making significant changes? Is it a buyer's market or a seller's market?

Finally, they are unsure if their children are interested in using any of the properties in the future. They could keep the properties for the kids but in the end they are not sure if anyone wants the property.

THE SOLUTIONS

At the risk of sounding like a broken record, there are two very important steps to take when you are dealing with real estate decisions: a) Spend time reflecting on the overall retirement vision (Chapter 1) and b) Don't do anything within the first two years of retirement (Chapter 3).

THE NEW CONDO

There are two key issues for this decision: timing and usage.

First, let's talk about the timing of this decision. Why is it so important that this decision be made today? If they purchase now, they will be able to customize the property to their likes. This property is being built in a favourable location. However, as Sam and Jennifer settle into their retirement years or as they age and become less mobile, they may find that this location is not as ideal as they would like. Therefore, when making this decision they should develop criteria based on their housing wants and needs, now and in the future, and rank the criteria in order of importance.

What would they list as the most important features and benefits of a new condo? In some ways this is a difficult question to answer if they are not entirely sure how their retirement years will evolve. This goes back to the all important "two year rule" (don't make any significant decisions in the first two years) and building the overall retirement vision. The criteria they put on the list two years from now may be very different from the list today.

In fact, the timing of this decision today relates to the schedule of the condo builder rather than Sam and Jennifer's schedule. Remember, there is nothing that is pushing them out of their current home. Rather, this opportunity is more of something that is pulling (or tempting) them out of their home.

It is also important to consider the timing of this decision as it relates to the age and cycle of the current real estate market. It may be disruptive to their retirement to buy into a new condo development only to have costs increase along the way while the market value declines. This situation could have an impact on their overall retirement lifestyle plans. With this in mind, is this a wise risk to take? Is it less risky to buy something that has already been built even if it requires some modifications?

Finally, one of the most important points to consider has to do with the use of the property. Even though Sam and Jennifer may not need the amount of space they have in their current home, this space will definitely come in handy when their children and grandchildren come to visit. For many grandparents, maintaining a space that is large enough to accommodate the kids and grandkids for family gatherings and special occasions is an extremely important part of their life. They want to encourage family get-togethers and want to have a space that is comfortable for the size of the group. They want to have a safe place for the grandkids to play and they also want to have enough space available to host sleepovers…the greatest fun a grandparent can have.

Sam and Jennifer have made a list of the things most important to them in their current life. At the top of this list is financial freedom, flexibility to travel over the next two to three years and spending time with the kids and grandkids. They are better able to do these things when they do not have the extra mortgage expense or condo fees. For the time being they have decided to remain in their current home. They will wait to see what the first two years of retirement bring; they will continue to watch out for opportunities to downsize profitably.

THE CURRENT HOME

The current home is a great storehouse of value. This value can be used to secure a line of credit that could be used to help finance a trip of a lifetime as well as unexpected medical needs that may arise.

Some people may enter retirement with a small mortgage. A mortgage payment is a combination of both principal and interest. Once you retire you may look for ways to reduce your monthly expenses. One way to reduce the monthly mortgage payment is to convert your mortgage to an "equity line of credit". By converting to an equity line of credit you will now be responsible for paying only the monthly interest costs on the outstanding debt. This gives you the flexibility to pay down the debt as you see fit. To do this, you will need to discuss this plan with your bank and then complete the appropriate paperwork. The interest costs are just a fraction of the total monthly payment. Many seniors may find that it is less expensive to stay in their current home than it is to move to an apartment or other assisted living environment.

THE FLORIDA HOME

Sam and Jennifer bought the Florida home 10 years ago. During this time they have traveled to Florida three to four times each year. Over the past few years they have been spending more time in Florida, but they are also becoming more and more interested in spending time elsewhere.

Sam and Jennifer have been thinking about renting their home to others on a week by week basis. Over time, if poor health restricts their ability to travel, they could rent out the home all year long or make the home available to other family and friends. They see this as an ideal investment that will be a great meeting place for all of their kids and grandkids for years to come. At this time they have no intention to sell; rather, they want to pass it on to the family, in some way, through their estate.

Since the property is located in Florida, Sam and Jennifer have several issues to address.

Sam and Jennifer must ensure they are not declared U.S. residents, or they will have to pay U.S. income tax on their worldwide income. To avoid being declared a U.S. resident, they must follow a wide range of criteria including being in the U.S. fewer than 183 days each year, maintaining their primary residence in Canada, maintaining bank accounts, automobile insurance and a driver's license in Canada, and having family primarily in Canada, to name a few. It is wise to receive professional advice on the tax consequences of owning foreign property well in advance of the purchase

A Canadian resident who owns property in Florida will be subject to a 30% withholding tax on any gross rental income received. Unfortunately, this tax is NOT reduced by the Canada – U.S. tax treaty. To avoid the 30% gross withholding tax they must file a U.S. tax return and elect to pay tax on the net rental income. The Canadian resident can then receive a refund for any taxes withheld; to the extent the withholding amount exceeds the tax payable. By filing a U.S. income tax return they can now apply expenses against the income received, thus reducing the 30% withholding tax. The U.S. tax regulations provide that if a tax return of a foreign national is not filed within 18 months of the original due date, the IRS will disallow all deductible expenses.

When selling the property, additional withholding taxes on the property may apply. A 10% withholding tax is typically applied to the sale of the property. This may be reduced or eliminated if the sale price is less than $300,000 and the property is sold to an individual who will use it as their principal residence, or where they are able to obtain a specific "withholding tax certificate" from the IRS.

Finally, upon death there could be some "double taxation" that takes place on the U.S. property in the estate. If the total estate value (from all Canadian and other worldwide assets) is greater than $2 million and the value of the total U.S. investments, real estate, business ventures, etc. exceed $60,000, then the estate tax may range from 25% to 45%. Not all of this tax can be applied against the same capital gains tax that is payable in Canada. Therefore, double taxation occurs. A Canadian citizen may be able to hold the real estate in a trust or holding company to reduce or avoid the U.S. estate taxes. If it is likely the U.S. real estate will form part of your estate, one must be pro-active in planning and obtain the advice of a professional in this area.

With these considerations in mind, Sam and Jennifer decided to hold a family meeting to discuss the long term benefits of owning the Florida property in perpetuity. Although their intent of passing the property to their children was well intended, the family agreed that the best course of action would be to first consult a professional and to assess the financial implications of their decisions. Based on this analysis, the family agreed that the best course of action will be to sell the property in the coming years to avoid unnecessary taxes.

The key point is to seek the advice of an expert in this area so that you know exactly the implications of each step you take.

THE COTTAGE

The value of the cottage has risen exponentially over the years and is now one of the family's most valuable assets. The home in the city has been subject to the typical ups and downs of the real estate market and has not seen the same degree of appreciation. If Sam and Jennifer sold the cottage today they would realize a significant amount of capital gains and would be subject to tax on these gains. If they sold the city house today, assuming that the gain on the value of the house is also taxable, the amount of capital gains tax to be paid would be substantially less.

When Sam and Jennifer reflect back on the timing of each purchase and the rate of appreciation in value of each property they see the following:

- They bought the cottage in 1975 for $50,000. From 1975 to 1998 the value of the cottage did not change that much. By 1998 they estimated the value of the cottage to be $75,000. However, between 1998 and 2008 the cottage has doubled in value three times. Today they estimate the value of the cottage to be $600,000. If they sold the cottage today the capital gains tax to be paid on the cottage would be approximately $110,000.

- They bought their current home in 1998 for $250,000 and may now sell it to purchase the new condo. Due to the fluctuations in the real estate market the value of their home is estimated today to be $300,000.

In Canada all home owners have access to a "tax-free" capital gains exemption on the value of their principal residence. For most people this means that any gain in the value of their home, between the time they bought it and the time they sell it, is tax-free.

According to Canadian tax law, for any property owned prior to 1972, no tax is payable on the gain in the value of that property. For any property owned between 1972 and 1981, each spouse can each own one property and have no tax applied to the capital gain of that property. From 1982 to the present, only one principal residence is allowed for each family (mom, dad and minor kids). The "principal residence exemption" from tax is declared at the time of sale of the property. It does not have to be declared in advance. As long as the property was lived in for some time each year, it can be claimed as the principal residence. If you used the property to generate rental income, it cannot be declared as a personal use property during that time and will not receive the exemption for this rental period.

The home in the city would typically be considered as the principal residence of the family and would not attract any tax on the sale of the property. Yet, it is possible to designate any property as the principal residence for any time period you choose. Only one property can be declared as the principal residence at any point in time. By applying this exemption strategically, significant amounts of tax can be avoided.

What should they do?

On the sale of the cottage, Sam and Jennifer could declare that the cottage has been their principal residence from 1998. This means that they have now sheltered the growth in the value of the cottage during this time and have potentially saved as much as $110,000 in taxes (assuming the cottage retains its value). They will have to pay approximately $10,000 in taxes based on the capital gain realized on the appreciation of the city home. That's a significant saving!

Sam and Jennifer have decided to spend more and more time at the cottage over the next 10 years. They feel that the demand for cottage property will continue and they believe that the size of the capital gain 10 years from now will far exceed the capital gain they may see on a new city condo. They have decided to declare their cottage as their principal residence as of 1998 and pay the tax on the appreciation of their city home when the home is sold.

Sam and Jennifer met with their tax advisor before making their decision to ensure they had everything well documented in the event the tax department questions the calculation of future capital gains.

IN SUMMARY

This chapter discussed different matters to consider with regard to your principal residence and your other real estate properties. Since the family home is often one of the largest assets owned, efficient planning on how the home equity can best be used is extremely important.

Your home and other properties can provide equity to fund an enhanced lifestyle, may be a less expensive alternative to moving into a condo or other residence and can be used to shelter capital gains. A U.S. property can provide you with equity but may also present a challenge because of different tax implications. It is recommended that you seek professional advice regarding any foreign properties.

Your home is definitely your castle and a financial fortress that can be used to fight any number of different income and tax related battles in retirement. It is an excellent source of tax-free value that can also be used to enhance your future lifestyle.

THINGS YOU NEED TO KNOW

- For most Canadians, their home is one of the largest assets.
- All Canadians have access to a "principal residence exemption". This exemption is applied at the time of the sale of the property and eliminates capital gains taxes owing on the property.
- Since 1982, the principal residence exemption is available to individuals or couples and not available to each spouse for two different properties.
- You can use the principal residence exemption on any property. This allows you to minimize capital gains taxes by applying the exemption to the property with the greatest capital gain.
- U.S. properties held by Canadian citizens potentially expose the Canadian to the U.S. residence rules, which may necessitate filing a U.S. tax return on their worldwide income.
- The Canadian principal residence exemption cannot be applied to a U.S. property.

- U.S. properties held by Canadian citizens may also be exposed to additional taxes for rental income received, capital gains taxes when sold or estate taxes on death. Some of these taxes are incurred more than once without offsetting credits. This means that you could be exposed to double taxation.

QUESTIONS YOU NEED TO ASK

- What will you use the home or property for?
- How frequently will you use the property?
- Is it large enough to host family functions?
- Do you need to generate income from this property?
- Is the home close to family, friends and the amenities that are important to you?
- Is it important to make a decision right now or is this a decision that can be delayed until the time is more favourable to act.

THINGS YOU NEED TO DO

- Track your "cost base" for all real estate properties including your city home. Even though you may assume that you will apply the principal residence exemption to your city home, you may change your mind in the future. Expenses incurred to upkeep the property can be used to reduce the size of the capital gain. **Keep all receipts.**
- Evaluate the return on your real estate investment. Is the money spent worth it as it relates to the costs incurred and the amount of time you use the property?

DECISIONS YOU NEED TO MAKE

- Is this a property that you expect to hold for life or sell at some point in the future?
- Discuss property issues with the entire family. Their input may help to make the decisions related to property, like the family cottage, that much easier.
- Are the added U.S. tax issues worth it in order to own U.S. real estate?

MASTER YOUR RETIREMENT
Your Home is Your Castle, and Don't Forget It!

TIPS

- For many Canadians the home is one of the largest assets they own. It is important to manage this asset as effectively as possible in retirement.

- Your principal residence can be used to provide tax-free income in retirement and can be used to keep taxable income below important tax rates and clawback zones.

- In some instances it may be more beneficial to stay in your home as long as you can even if you have a mortgage. The mortgage, if converted to an interest only line of credit, may cost you less than a new apartment or senior care facility.

- When considering a new home, consider space in the home to accommodate your children and grandchildren on special occasions.

- Be aware of the additional taxes and risks that come from owning U.S. property.

- When downsizing and moving to a new home, try to do so in such a way that you do not end up with a mortgage.

- Discussing the use, upkeep and future ownership of a cottage, family condo or other real estate with your children. This will help you make any final decisions and help maintain family harmony.

TRAPS

- You do not need to declare your "principal residence election" until the time the property is sold. With 20 – 20 hindsight you can decide whether your home in the city or your cottage has the greatest unrealized capital gain, and thus the greatest potential tax liability.

- When considering moving to a condo, 55 plus or seniors residence, do so in your time frame and on your terms. Do not rush with this important decision.

- Postpone any substantial decisions until after the first two years of retirement. During the first two years you will settle in to a new routine which may influence who you'd like to live close to and the amenities you'd like to have close by.

CHAPTER 6

Believe It or Not, the Taxman is Your Very Best Friend!

Personal development is your springboard to personal excellence. Ongoing, continuous, non-stop personal development literally assures you that there is no limit to what you can accomplish. BRIAN TRACY

Stan and Jane Milner don't understand how Terry and Trish do it. They don't understand how they can take the types of trips they take. They don't understand how they can afford the things they do. As two retired couples it has become challenging for Stan and Jane to keep up with Terry and Trish.

What makes this situation really hard to understand is that Stan and Terry worked together, doing the same job and with the same employer for the last 20 years. They earned the same income, but for some reason Terry and Trish seem to have the better lifestyle. Stan and Jane know Terry and Trish well enough that if they had received an inheritance, they would know about it.

So what is the difference? Are Terry and Trish just that much better at managing their money? Have they had better luck with their investments over the years? Are they living on more credit than Stan and Jane? Or is it something completely different?

THE ISSUES

Stan and Jane and Terry and Trish have the same resources and the same income. The only difference between the two couples is the way in which each is filing their respective tax returns. Today Terry and Trish are 65 and reaping the benefits of some significant tax changes affecting retired people in Canada. Just a few years ago, as they were planning their retirement, these same benefits did not exist.

In their situation today, the amount of tax payable each year has been reduced by as much as 35% while their after-tax spendable income has increased by 14%. Over the next 20 years, this could lead to a total tax saving of as much as $131,841 and as much as $172,833 in additional after-tax income to spend.

Terry and Trish have been on top of these changes and have thus reaped the benefits. Stan and Jane don't like dealing with their investments and their taxes so they avoid these subjects at all cost and are thus unaware of these changes.

Terry and Trish are pro-actively managing their taxes. Are you?

When it comes to retirement most of the attention is placed on investment returns and the amount of money you have saved for retirement. The most common question asked is: "Do I have enough?" Much attention is placed on gross before tax income and not enough attention is placed on after-tax income. As mentioned previously, it matters not what you have, it only matters what you keep.

If you could reduce your taxes by effectively "managing" the tax return, this could be the equivalent of either increasing the rate of return on your investments by 25% to 60% or increasing the amount of investment capital by the same amount. It is critical to understand the available tax credits, clawback zones and your personal marginal tax rates to efficiently manage your after tax income.

- Are you aware of the three core income benchmarks? Do you manage your investments, income and taxes accordingly to stay within these benchmarks?

- To reap your maximum Canada Pension Plan benefit you must consider three steps. Do you know what they are?
- Do you know how to maximize your benefits by understanding how Old Age Security works?
- Do you understand pension income splitting and to apply it on your tax return?

THE SOLUTIONS

Why is Tax Return Management so Important?

Old Age Security is a government benefit program that begins to be "clawed back" once your income begins to exceed $65,000 (in 2008). This amount is clawed back on your tax return by 15% per year. For every dollar of income earned above $65,000, you will have to pay back 15%. This is not a good thing and should be avoided where at all possible. Why would you ever want to give money back to the government?

To emphasize this point, let's look at an example. Assume you have a $250,000 RRIF portfolio whereby you draw a conservative income equivalent to 5% of the value of the portfolio. 5% of $250,000 is $12,500 of taxable income. Let's assume your total before tax annual retirement income today is $65,000.

If the $12,500 of investment income was in addition to the $65,000 of income you already receive, you would be subject to the equivalent of a 46% to 48% tax (marginal tax rate + the Old Age Security clawback) on this additional $12,500 of income. This means that you would see a whopping $6,000 of your $12,500 earned income disappear in taxes and clawbacks.

Alternatively, what if you could access this same amount of income in such a way that you would not pay any tax at all? If the current return is $12,500 and the money that you saved by avoiding the clawback is another $6,000, when we add the two together we see a total benefit of $18,500. For the sake of our example, if you were able to draw the equivalent of $18,500 of income from your $250,000 investment portfolio, your rate of return would be 7.4% (i.e.: $18,500 divided by $250,000 = 7.4%). By increasing your return from 5% to 7.4% you have, in effect, increased your rate of return by 48% without increasing the level of risk in your portfolio. If you could increase your rate of return by 48% without taking on more risk…would you? Of course you would!

Therefore, focusing only on your gross (before tax) rate of return is futile. **It only matters what income you keep.** Therefore, efficient tax return management is a core component of Mastering Your Retirement.

Another way to look at the impact of tax efficiency is by thinking of it as increasing the size of your investment portfolio. How much investment capital would you need to earn $18,500 of income? Assuming we continue to draw income from the portfolio at a conservative rate of 5% per year, to generate $18,500 of income you would need to have $370,000 of investment capital. By focusing on greater tax efficiency you are in effect increasing the size of your portfolio from $250,000 to $370,000. By focusing on greater tax efficiency you are increasing the size of your portfolio by virtually 48%!

If you could increase the size of your investment portfolio, virtually instantly, from $250,000 to $370,000…would you do it?

If you could increase the size of your portfolio without having to take on more risk…would you do it?

If you could increase the rate of return on your investment portfolio by 48% without taking on more risk…would you do it?

Of course you would!

Tax return management is extremely important. Tax return management is one of the key cornerstones of Mastering Your Retirement. Instead of chasing investment returns in volatile markets, keep your portfolio simple and secure. The returns you seek may be on your tax form, not necessarily in your investment account.

THE THREE TENORS OF
AFTER-TAX INCOME PLANNING

We know that in the opera world the "Three Tenors" made beautiful music together. In the same way we have the "Three Tenors" of the tax system. Each tenor represents one of three important ranges in the tax system. These are the benchmarks in which to stay within to optimize your tax efficiency. All other planning around the portfolio stems from the management of the tax return.

Let's begin by determining the desired amount of after-tax monthly income for you and your spouse:

- Tenor #1: Are you in the $4,550 club?
- Tenor #2: Are you in the $8,345 club?
- Tenor #3: Are you above the $8,345 club?

Each of these three levels represents a key turning point on the tax return for the couple who is age 65 and older. If you are younger than age 65, you want to keep these income goals in mind when making decisions about how and when to draw your CPP, how and when to draw your RRSP investments, severance payments and the structure of your investment portfolio. Age 65 is a critical juncture that we need to plan ahead for.

The $4,550 Club

Will you be earning $4,550 per month (or less) after-tax, in retirement? Can you support your lifestyle on $4,550 per month or less? This is the combined after-tax income amount for both you and your spouse, in a highly efficient retirement income portfolio.

This income level is based on two equal incomes of $30,000 or less in retirement. This income level maximizes the "Age Credit" and the "Pension Credit" available to Canadians today.

To put this into perspective, to generate the same $4,550 per month after-tax, two individuals would need to earn approximately $34,000 each (instead of $30,000 each) or one person would have to earn the equivalent of $71,000 as a pre-retirement income. The fact that two equal incomes of $30,000 generates the same after tax income in retirement as two $34,000 incomes or one $71,000 (pre-retirement), illustrates the benefit of the income splitting provision as well as the pension and age credits.

Once you earn more than $4,550 after-tax per month, you will enter into a higher tax bracket and the age credit will begin to be clawed back. The next $10,000 drawn in income would see a tax rate of approximately 30% applied to each dollar of income. Structuring your lifestyle or your investments to ensure your income does not exceed $30,000 each is highly tax efficient.

The $8,345 Club

What if you need more income than $4,550 after-tax per month? What is the next major obstacle to tax efficiency? The answer is $8,345 per month after-tax. This figure represents two before-tax incomes of $65,000 or less. This is the equivalent of two pre-retirement incomes of approximately $70,000 or one individual income of $153,000.

This is the point in which Old Age Security begins to be "clawed back". In 2008 the clawback rate for Old Age Security was 15% for every dollar of taxable income earned above $64,718. Old Age Security, for those age 65 and older, is approximately $500 per month per spouse. Over a 20 year period of time, $500 per month per spouse is the equivalent of $240,000 of income paid to you from the Federal Government during retirement. Looking back at our previous example of an investment portfolio of $250,000, the Federal Government is in effect giving you an additional $240,000 to live on. This is virtually doubling the size of your investment portfolio.

Do we say "No Thanks" to this income?

What if much of this amount was actually a refund of all of the tax money you've paid to the government over your lifetime? Would you take this source of income more seriously? Sure you would.

So why would you want to do anything that would potentially reduce the amount received from the Federal Government? What if this were called the "tax payback program"? Would you NOT wish to take back some of the taxes you paid during your lifetime? Of course! So why would you want to dismiss the Old Age Security benefit prematurely?

$8,345 per month after-tax is the amount you would receive after-tax based on two equal $65,000 incomes. This is the equivalent of two pre-retirement incomes of approximately $70,000 or one individual income of $153,000.

On the next $10,000 of taxable income drawn (above $65,000) the effective tax rate would be a very significant 60%! The tax rate is this high because it is a combination of the normal taxes owing plus the 15% clawback rate.

Here's the question: What do you need to do to keep your lifestyle and/or taxable income received below $65,000 (each)?

Do you need to adjust your expenses? Do you need to reduce your RRIF income or RRSP savings? Do you need to add more money to other "tax efficient" investments?

The likely answer is "all of the above", this is why tax return management is so important.

The $8,345+ Club

Do you need to have more than $8,345 per month after-tax? If so, your objective is to ensure the income drawn is highly tax efficient. In other words, in an ideal world, you would want to receive the income, yet not pay tax on the income.

In the previous chapter we talked about how the equity in your principal residence is tax-free. If you are already at the $65,000 income level and need an additional $4,000 of after-tax income, if you draw this money from your RRSP/RRIF you will need to withdraw $10,000 to end up with $4,000 you can spend. Alternatively, if you draw $4,000 from your investment account (assuming all of the tax has been paid on this investment) or the equity in your home (where there will be no tax paid on this withdrawal) then you will pay no tax on this income while saving $6,000 of valuable capital.

If you are in this category, the reality is you may have to payback the Old Age Security amount you receive. However, if it is at all possible, plan your investments, real estate and your income in such a way that your taxable income does not exceed $65,000 (each) per year.

CANADA PENSION PLAN

There are three key concepts to consider with regard to your Canada Pension Plan retirement benefit.

1. **Maximize your benefits:** When calculating your Canada Pension Plan benefit, the Federal Government will take into account the number of your working years. If you were out of the workforce for a period of time these years will be included in your calculation and thus reduce the total benefits to be paid to you. You can request to have those years removed from your pension income calculation if you were out of the workforce due to time spent raising children. This is called the Child Rearing Provision. Review your CPP statement to ensure it is accurate and to ensure that the years in which you did not contribute are eliminated from the calculation. To do this, contact the Service Canada office nearest you and ask for an updated CPP printout, review it and then discuss it with one of the representatives to ensure you are receiving the maximum benefit available to you.

2. **Begin benefits at age 60 or 65?** Many people believe it is better to wait until 65 to begin collecting CPP benefits, because the monthly amount will be greater. As discussed in Chapter 2, if you retired at age 60 but did not take your CPP income benefit until age 65, it would not be until approximately age 77 to 80 that you would be further ahead. Therefore, we encourage people to typically draw their CPP pension income benefit at age 60 or as soon after as they can. Each situation is unique, but this is a good rule of thumb to follow.

3. **Split your CPP Pension Income Benefit with your spouse:**
   Depending on your specific situation, it may be beneficial to split
   some of your CPP pension income benefit with your spouse. To
   do so you need to apply to CPP to have this election completed
   for you. In general, you have the ability to combine your two
   pension amounts together and then divide the two equally so
   each spouse receives the same amount. Note that in some cases,
   due to the approach used by CPP, you may not end up with
   exactly equal amounts.

   Canada Pension Plan will continue to pay a monthly benefit to a
   surviving spouse and to minor age children in the event of death.
   The amount received is based on the age of the survivors. Canada
   Pension Plan will also pay a lump sum death benefit of $2,500.
   This death benefit is taxable income in the estate.

OLD AGE SECURITY

This is a government funded program available to all Canadians age 65
and over who have lived in Canada a minimum of 10 years. It is important to note that Old Age Security is different from the Canada Pension
Plan. During your employment years you and your employer each
contributed to the Canada Pension Plan. The amount of Canada Pension
Plan benefit you receive today is based on those contributions. However,
Old Age Security is funded from the general tax revenues of the Federal
Government and is the same for everyone who qualifies. The amount
you receive is indexed with inflation every three months. In the fourth
quarter of 2008, the Old Age Security benefit was $516.96 per month.
This income is fully taxable.

Old Age Security is exactly that. It is meant to provide additional
financial security in retirement. Therefore, if you earn too much taxable
income in retirement you will have to pay some of it back. The current
threshold is $64,718 per couple. Any taxable income earned above this
amount will trigger, on your tax return, a repayment of 15% of every
dollar earned above this threshold. For example, $10,000 of additional
taxable income above $64,718 will require $1,500 to be paid back to the
Federal Government.

Over 20 years of retirement, the amount of Old Age Security received can add up to a significant amount of money. A benefit of $500 per month for each spouse = $1,000 per month = $12,000 per year. Over 20 years of retirement this adds up to $240,000.

The clawback threshold is indexed with inflation and will usually increase by 1% to 2% each year, which is beneficial. However, since the inflation number will change each year, the prudent citizen who is Mastering . Retirement will want to keep track of this figure and plan their income wisely throughout each year.

TAX CREDITS

A tax credit is a calculation that directly reduces the amount of tax paid, as opposed to a tax deduction which reduces taxable income (e.g.: an RRSP contribution). A tax credit of $5,000 is multiplied by 15% to equal $750. If your tax owing before the credit is claimed is $2,000; after the credit is claimed your tax owing will be only $1,250. Tax credits are highly advantageous.

The most common tax credits are (all figures are for the 2008 tax year):

- **Personal exemption:** All tax filers receive a basic personal exemption from tax on the first $9,600 of annual income. This amount is indexed with inflation. If one spouse does not have any income and you are unable to split some of your income with this individual, a spousal credit for this amount will be added to your personal exemption amount.

- **Age amount:** Available to those over age 65 with less than $31,524 in income (note: this amount is indexed and changes annually). The credit is currently $5,276 for each spouse meeting the criteria. This is the equivalent of approximately $1,500 in reduced taxes each and every year in retirement. Over 20 years the tax savings add up to $30,000. NOTE: The age credit begins to be clawed back at a rate of 15% each year when your income exceeds the $31,524 amount.

- **Pension income amount:** The first $2,000 of pension income is tax-free for each spouse. This is the equivalent of $600 in tax credits each and every year in retirement, over 20 years this will result in approximately $12,000 in tax savings for the couple. This amount is not clawed back.

- **Caregiver amount:** Do you take care of an adult who is infirm and dependent on you? Does this person reside with you? If so, you may be eligible to claim a "caregiver" tax credit. If the dependent's income exceeds $18,082 (indexed with inflation) the credit will be zero.

- **Infirm dependent amount:** In the event you are taking care of another adult individual who is unable to care for themselves due to a permanent mental or physical disability, you may claim some of these expenses as part of the Infirm Dependent tax credit. The amount of credit available is $4,095.

- **Disability tax credit:** The maximum credit available to a disabled person is $7,021. The application for this credit requires certification from a medical practitioner.

- **Medical expenses:** The credit is based on the taxpayer's allowable medical expenses for any 12-month period ending in the year minus 3% of the taxpayer's net income on line 236 (up to an annually indexed maximum amount). Because the claim is reduced by 3% of the taxpayer's net income, it is often best to claim the amount on the return of the lower-income taxpayer, unless that taxpayer is not taxable

- **Charitable donations:** The first $200 of total charitable gifts is eligible for a 15% Federal credit and the remainder of the gifts is eligible for a 29% Federal tax credit. When combined with the Provincial credits these amounts add up to your marginal tax rate. You may carry forward donations for five years and by doing may receive better tax treatment for your donations.

MARGINAL TAX RATES

To maximize the amount of income you keep, stay under specific Marginal Tax Rates. In Canada, at certain income levels, every additional dollar we earn is taxed at a higher rate.

The Federal Government charges tax based on the following income levels:

2007 and after	Rate
Up to $37,885	15%
$37,886 to $75,769	22%
$75,770 to $123,184	26%
Over $123,184	29%

Each Provincial Government has its own marginal tax rate levels as well. For example, in Ontario the marginal tax rates are:

2008 Bracket	Rate
$0 to 36.020	6.05%
$36,021 to $72,041	9.15%
Over $72,041	11.16%

When these two tables are combined, the marginal tax rates for an Ontario resident are:

Up to $9,600	0%
$9,600 to $36,020	21.05%
$36,021 to $37,885	24.15%
$37,886 to $72,041	31.00%
$72,042 to $75,769	33.16%
$75,770 to $123,184	37.16%
$123,185+	40.16%

Why is this important? Before you draw your next dollar of income you need to be aware if you are entering into a new level of tax. This may influence when you draw this money, the source from which it is taken and the amount of income you draw.

DIFFERENT INVESTMENT INCOME IS TAXED DIFFERENTLY

Did you know that different types of income are taxed differently?

Interest income earned from a bond, GIC or bank account is taxed at the same rates as if you had earned this income in your job. This is the highest level of tax on any type of investment income.

Alternatively, tax paid on a dividend received from a stock or capital gains tax paid on the growth of an investment (when it is sold) is taxed at a much lower rate.

Example #1: In Ontario, you will pay zero tax on any dividends paid so long as your total income is less than $32,000 (approximately). In British Columbia this figure is closer to $72,000.

Example #2: If your total earned income is currently $50,000, and you were to draw another $15,000 of investment income you would pay different amounts of tax based on the type of income received. If this is interest income, the tax rate would be approximately 31% (i.e.: 31% of the amount you received would disappear in taxes). If this were dividend income, the tax rate would be approximately 9% whereas if this were considered to be 100% capital gains, it would be taxed at approximately 16%.

Warning: When dividends are taxed they are first increased by a certain multiple and then given a tax credit. The net effect is a tax rate of 9% in this example. However, due to the increase that is applied, it is this increased amount that is added to your income and may thus put your total taxable income above $65,000 and into the OAS clawback zone. This is something that is very important to watch out for and to avoid; your tax professional can provide you with detailed information.

This information is extremely important for two reasons:

- To remain within your most appropriate or tax efficient income level (as described previously) you may need to strategically draw one type of income over another.

- To give you the flexibility to efficiently manage your tax return, it may be prudent to build up investments outside of your RRSP. For those individuals who expect to have greater than $4,250 in after-tax income per month at age 65, it is increasingly important to have some non-registered investments accumulated for your use. For those individuals who will have greater than $8,345 per month in after-tax income it is imperative that you have a substantial amount of non-registered investments to keep your annual taxable income below this threshold, by drawing down your capital.

INCOME SPLITTING

Based on each of the previous points, when tax is minimized and credits are maximized you can have two lower and equal incomes in retirement. The goal is to have an equal income for each spouse.

In 2007, the Federal Government introduced the ability for Canadian retirees to share up to 50% of eligible pension income with their spouse.

Example #1: At age 60, one spouse can share up to 50% of the value of their monthly pension income with their spouse. If this pension income was $3,000 per month, up to $1,500 per month could be transferred to the tax return of the other spouse. This not only reduces the total amount of potential tax paid on this income, but it also increases the benefit received from both the pension credit and the age credit.

Example #2: At age 65, one spouse can share up to 50% of the value of their RRIF income with their spouse, achieving the same benefits as noted in the previous paragraph.

Example #3: The eligible amount of income that can be split is up to 50%, giving you the ability to determine what this amount should be at the end of each tax year. Did you get that? You make this determination not in advance, but only once you see your overall tax picture *at the end of* the year. Wow! This is very powerful because it gives you the chance to take into consideration all other non-splittable income received for each spouse. In the event that one spouse receives considerable taxable investment income, they can reduce their total income and tax owing by transferring up to 50% of their pension income to their spouse. This is a significant benefit that can save you tens of thousands of dollars throughout your retirement.

PRIVATE PENSION INCOME OPTIONS

For many people, the opportunity to gradually retire is the ideal approach. However, if you slow down and work part time, the question is: where does the balance of your income come from? Can you work part time and draw some pension income? Can you do so while continuing to work for the same firm and thus continue to make pension contributions based on your reduced salary?

The answer to these questions is: Yes! This is great news because it gives you greater flexibility for retirement and for structuring your income in the most tax efficient manner.

If an employee is at least 55, he/she can draw up to 60% of the benefits accrued in the pension plan while continuing to accumulate benefits based on current employment. No conditions are imposed on whether the employee works part- or full-time. However, this ability to draw a pension while continuing to accrue benefits will not be extended to designated plans (more commonly called top-hat plans), which cover only one employee or a small group of highly compensated individuals.

IN SUMMARY

In this chapter we discussed nine issues that can contribute to greater tax efficiency and thus increase your after-tax income quite substantially. Tax return management is a significant component of your retirement income planning process as it will influence how you build your investment portfolio.

Is this time well spent? Based on the case study at the beginning of this chapter you can see the significant difference in taxes paid and after-tax income received.

Remember, it is not your gross investment return or your gross income that matters most in retirement. The only thing that matters is the income you keep: after-tax, after-fees and after-inflation.

THINGS YOU NEED TO KNOW

- Tax return management should influence the design of your investment portfolio.
- Tax return management should influence how and when you draw income.
- Managing your tax return is about understanding the marginal tax rate levels for your province, the clawback zones and how different investment income is taxed.
- Old Age Security is one of the single largest government benefits you could receive in retirement. Your total benefits could be close to $240,000 of additional income throughout your retirement years (based on two people over 20 years).
- There are three key after-tax income levels to watch out for: less than $4,550, less than $8,345 and greater than $8,345 per month.
- Be familiar with credits available to help you reduce tax.

QUESTIONS YOU NEED TO ASK

- How much after-tax income do I (we) need to live on each month?
- What are the marginal rate zones in Canada? In my province?
- Which of the three tax zones am I in today?
- What is my ideal tax zone (to reduce taxes and/or clawbacks)?
- Are we taking advantage of all of the available tax credits?
- Do I need to restructure my current portfolio design and income strategy so as to reduce my tax payable?

THINGS YOU NEED TO DO

- Review your last two years of tax returns to assess if you have missed claiming certain credits. If you have, refile your returns.
- With your advisors, discuss and review alternative ways by which you can draw income from your investment portfolio to reduce taxes on the tax return.
- Plan ahead by looking at where you are investing money today. If you continue to add to your RRSP investments are you inviting the OAS clawback to appear?

DECISIONS YOU NEED TO MAKE

- Identify the income you need to cover basic living expenses as well as enhanced lifestyle expenses (Chapter 2).
- Categorize your income into monthly and annual expenses.
- Determine which "Tenor" club you fit into today.
- Decide which "Tenor" club you wish to be in tomorrow and in the future.
- Educate yourself on the tax credits and clawback zones.
- Adjust your portfolio structure to meet your income needs in the most tax efficient manner.

MASTER YOUR RETIREMENT
Believe It or Not, the Taxman is Your Very Best Friend!

TIPS

- Taxes, fees and inflation are three of your greatest enemies in retirement. Pay attention to these three on a regular basis.
- Different advisors, due to their education, experience and category of license will have access to different types of products. If your current advisor does not have the product you are looking for, ask around and seek it out.

TRAPS

- Don't accept your situation as it is, do everything possible to manage your tax return to its greatest level of efficiency.

CHAPTER 7

Taming the Risk and Return of Your Investment Portfolio

When you discover your mission, you will feel its demand. It will fill you with enthusiasm and a burning desire to get to work on it. W. CLEMENT STONE

James and Jennifer have retired. James sold his business recently and they now have a $1.5 million investment portfolio. $500,000 of this amount is invested in RRSP and $1 million is in non-registered investments.

James and Jennifer are worried about their portfolio. Now that they are retired, they are relying on the performance of the portfolio for their long term financial security, yet, they are concerned about the typical ups and downs of the equity market. They are concerned about the possibility of losing money.

Even though James did well in business, he has never been that comfortable investing in the stock market. It was one thing to control the risk of his business, it is something else to rely on others to manage the risk of the stock market.

THE ISSUES

There are many issues for James and Jennifer to consider as it relates to the risks, returns and the management of their portfolio.

They are now vulnerable to the highs and lows of the stock market. If they do not invest in the stock market, will the value of their portfolio decline in value due to the effects of inflation? The rates of return available from guaranteed investments such as a GIC are low. The economy is uncertain today. Will the economy remain slow or will it begin to grow again and when?

At a time in their life when they are excited about the future and looking forward to a new stage of life together, James and Jennifer have serious concerns.

There are three questions James and Jennifer wish to answer:

1. What is a realistic rate of return on their investments?
2. How much risk do they have to take to achieve this return?
3. What are the traits of an ideal investment?

James and Jennifer are looking for answers so that they can feel confident about the future.

THE SOLUTIONS

Now that you have determined your retirement vision, after-tax income objectives and optimized your tax return, it is time to turn your attention to your investment portfolio. The challenge with investing is that it is a complex, imperfect process. This chapter will emphasize several important components to building and evaluating portfolios. The foundation to this is the clear understanding of both risk and return.

UNDERSTANDING LONG TERM AVERAGE PORTFOLIO RETURNS

What is a reasonable annual rate of return? Is it 5%, 7%, 10%? To answer this question, let's focus on the long term average rates of return of different types of portfolios over different periods of time. We focus on portfolios because our objective is to produce the highest possible return with the least amount of risk.

Considerable research has been conducted on this subject over the past 50 years. Building an efficient portfolio is similar to cooking a meal. Each new ingredient added, and the amount that is added, will either greatly improve or greatly detract from the quality of the meal. The same is true for an efficient portfolio. Each new investment added to the port-folio, and the amount of money placed into that investment, will either add or subtract risk while adding or subtracting return. The objective is to hold a blend of different investments that produce the greatest return with the least amount of risk.

To understand long term average returns let's look at three sample efficient portfolios that have three different levels of risk: a conservative portfolio, a balanced portfolio and a growth portfolio.

	Conservative	Balanced	Growth
Canadian Bonds*	65%	50%	35%
Canadian Equities**	18%	25%	33%
Global Equities***	17%	25%	32%

   * The Scotia Capital Broad Market Bond Index for Canadian bonds.
  ** The Toronto Stock Exchange Composite Index for Canadian stocks.
*** The Morgan Stanley Composite Index (in Canadian dollars) for global equities.

The above table describes three common portfolios: conservative, balanced and growth. In general each portfolio would have three components: bonds, Canadian equities and global equities. The bonds are the "defensive" side of the portfolio. That is why the Conservative portfolio has almost twice the amount of bonds (65%) as does the Growth portfolio (35%). The Equities component is the exposure to the stock market. Exposure to the stock market can be gained by investing in individual stocks or through other types of investments such as mutual funds. In general, we believe it is beneficial to divide your exposure to the stock market by investing half into Canadian equities and half into global equities.

When you begin to invest, you first need to focus on the amount of risk you are willing to accept. Do you wish to have a low amount of risk? If so, you are a "conservative" investor. Are you comfortable with a high amount of risk? If so, then you are a "growth" investor. Do you wish to take a middle of the road approach? If so, you are a balanced investor.

With this understanding, what has been the short, medium and long term rate of return for these three different types of portfolios?

The long term compound annual rate of return for these three portfolios is as follows. For comparison purposes, we will also look at the return of the Toronto Stock Exchange (TSX):

TABLE 1: Annual Rate of Return

	Last 3 Years	Last 5 Years	Last 10 Years	Last 15 Years	Last 20 Years	Last 25 Years
Conservative	5.5%	7.3%	5.3%	7.8%	8.6%	9.8%
Balanced	6.2%	8.1%	4.9%	8.0%	8.5%	9.9%
Growth	7.0%	9.1%	4.7%	8.2%	8.5%	10.0%
TSX	16.2%	18.2%	9.0%	11.1%	10.0%	10.1%

Source: MorningStar PalTrak software for data ending June 30th, 2008.

What is a realistic rate of return expectation?

- A Conservative Portfolio (65% in bonds, 35% in equities): 5% to 7%.
- A Balanced Portfolio (50% in bonds, 50% in equities): 6% to 8%.
- A Growth Portfolio (35% in bonds, 65% in equities): 7% to 9%.

It is very important to understand that the rate of return for these types of investment categories will NEVER be the same year after year. There will be times when the returns for each of these categories will be higher and there will be times when they will be lower than the averages shown here. For 2008 and 2009 the expectation is that the returns will be lower than these averages.

You should know how to measure your current asset mix and how to measure the risk profile of your investment portfolio.

How to Measure Your Current Asset Mix

To measure your current asset mix, look at your investment statement. If you hold mutual funds, these funds will typically be described as a "bond" fund or an "equity" fund. These are the easy ones to categorize. Next you may see investments on your statement that are categorized as "balanced" funds or "asset allocation" funds. To be conservative, you should assume that 40% of the balanced fund is "defensive" while 60% is "equity". Balanced funds themselves are not necessarily conservative even though they may be described in that manner. You may see investments that are categorized as "income" investments. These are typically investments that can be found in the defensive/bond-like category but they may be the most aggressive in that category. Investments in this category can also be highly risky in that they can rise by as much as +20% and fall by as much as -20% in any given year. Don't be complacent and feel that you have a conservative portfolio if 40% or 60% of your holdings are in these types of investments.

If you hold a number of "individual" securities in your portfolio you may need your investment advisor to help you categorize these investments in terms of risk. Once again, even though you may hold two individual stocks in your portfolio they may not be of similar risk.

To assess your current asset mix, use this process and work with your advisor to determine your mix of investments. You will then understand if your current portfolio is conservative, balanced or growth oriented.

You must not look at returns in isolation. In fact, rate of return is one of the last things to consider before purchasing an investment. The most important issue to consider is the amount of "risk" you must endure to achieve a particular return.

UNDERSTANDING SHORT TERM VOLATILITY AND RISK

There are two sides to every investment: return and risk. It is easy to focus on returns, and when returns are good, volatility in returns or risk seems almost irrelevant. However, there is always a time throughout a typical market cycle where risk is the more dominant component of the investing equation. In 2008 all of the gains of the last 4 to 5 years were erased in a matter of months.

The challenge is how to quantify risk?

Risk can be measured by a calculation known as "standard deviation". Let's look at the long term annual "standard deviation" for the Toronto Stock Exchange. It will help us answer the question about risk. This is a very important concept as you will see in the next section.

To measure risk we begin with the long term rate of return. From Table 1, the Toronto Stock Exchange produced an average annual return of 10.1% over the past 25 years. To achieve this return you had to take some risk. Just how much risk? Over the past 25 years the standard deviation of the Toronto Stock Exchange is 14.6.

If we add and subtract the standard deviation from the average return we see that 66% of the time the annual rate of return was between -4.5% and +24.7%. (10.1% + 14.6 = 24.7%; 10.1% - 14.6 = -4.5%.) In the vast majority of one year periods the annual rate of return was quite acceptable for most people.

However, what about the other 34% of the time? The good news is that half of this time the returns were even better than the +24.7% noted above. The bad news is that 17% of the time the one year returns were worse than -4.5%. This is what is referred to as the "Red Zone". The "Red Zone" represents those historical one year returns that would typically occur once every 5 years. Just how bad did they get? If we subtracted the standard deviation figure two more times from -4.5% we would see that there were occasions where the 1 year return was as low as -33.7%.

To truly understand risk, it is important to consider the Red Zone.

Let's take a look at the Red Zone for our three sample portfolios.

TABLE 2: Annual Standard Deviation

	Last 3 Years	Last 5 Years	Last 10 Years	Last 15 Years	Last 20 Years	Last 25 Years
Conservative	3.6	3.5	5.5	5.9	6.2	6.5
Balanced	4.7	4.5	7.2	7.2	7.5	7.8
Growth	5.9	5.6	8.9	8.6	8.8	9.2
TSX	11.3	10.3	16.0	14.9	14.1	14.6

Here are the results for the Red Zone over the past 15 years follows:

- The Conservative Portfolio: The bottom 17% of returns were between -4% and -10% in any one year.

- The Balanced Portfolio: The bottom 17% of returns were between -6.4% and -13.6% in any one year.

- The Growth Portfolio: The bottom 17% of returns were between -9.0% and -17% in any one year.

- The Toronto Stock Exchange: The bottom 17% of returns were between -18.7% and -33.6%.

As you can see, a portfolio is defined, not by its return, but by its degree of risk 17% of the time. In moving from "conservative" to "growth" the downside risk becomes greater and greater. That is why it is critical to understand the asset mix of your portfolio and the degree of downside risk (as measured by three standard deviations from the average return).

In your younger years, as you were building your wealth, you could sustain these downturns and keep on investing. Now that you are close to or are in retirement, protecting capital and purchasing power is of paramount importance. Before considering any investment you must consider the downside risk. It is extremely important to recognize that even the most conservative portfolio can lose money.

How do you know what level of risk is right for you?

How do You Determine the Standard Deviation of Your Current Portfolio?

Many financial software programs can calculate this figure for you. It is also a calculation that is found on many mutual fund company websites. It is important to note that the "standard deviation" of your overall portfolio is NOT the sum of the weighted average of the standard deviation for each investment.

The best resource you have to discuss your portfolio risk with is your financial advisor.

What Level of Risk is Right For You?

There are three ways to determine the level of risk that is right for you:

1. Determine the amount of investment income you wish to draw from your portfolio (your variable sources of income).
2. Determine your personal comfort level with risk.
3. Consider where we are in the economic cycle.

Determine the Amount Of Investment Income You Wish to Draw From Variable Sources

In previous chapters we talked about the difference between guaranteed vs. variable sources of income as well as basic income needs vs. additional lifestyle wants. It is recommended that you cover your basic income needs with your guaranteed sources of income. Your lifestyle wants may be quite small or they may be quite significant. If the income required to cover the lifestyle wants is small, you may wish to take more risk with your investment portfolio. If your lifestyle wants are significant and you require a large amount of income to come from your investments, you may wish to be more conservative. The answer to this question will also depend on the size of your portfolio.

Amount of Income	Size of Portfolio	Action
Small	Large	You can take more risk because you can recover from a downturn. This would probably be more tax efficient as well.
Small	Small	You will likely wish to have a more conservative portfolio.
Large	Small	You will want to be more conservative.
Large	Large	You will want to be more conservative.

Did the last point sound counter-intuitive to you? If you need more income why would you not take on more risk? After all, to produce a higher return you need to take on more risk.

Let's reflect on the information learned earlier. Taking on more risk to generate a higher return will run the risk of encountering back to back years of significant negative returns. The negative return combined with the income withdrawal will significantly reduce the capital. It is possible that you may never earn this capital back and it will be lost forever. The income earned on this smaller amount of money will not cover your lifestyle income wants in the future. In an effort to meet your income wants, you have taken more risk only to end up with depleted capital. For some people, this has occurred in the first 2 to 3 years of their retirement, forever impacting their long term lifestyle options.

Is today the right time to retire? If you invest conservatively, can you cover your "lifestyle income wants" based on the current size of your portfolio? If the answer is yes, you know you can retire now. If the answer is no, you may need to buy a lifetime annuity (to create more income and more guarantees), reduce your "income wants", postpone your preferred retirement date and/or invest more money before you retire.

This type of analysis is referred to as "calculating your financial risk capacity" or your ability to recover from market volatility.

Are You Ready to Take on the Emotional Risks?

Do you understand your own personal financial risk profile? Ask your advisor to help you determine your comfort level with volatility and thus your ideal portfolio design. Based on your emotional comfort level with risk and volatility (can you sleep at night during volatile periods of time) you may find that at this stage in your life you are looking for a portfolio where 17% of the worst returns are no worse than -5%. Your financial advisor should develop such a portfolio for you, and then explain to you, why and how they constructed this recommended portfolio.

To determine if today is the right day to retire, return to the first section in this chapter that discusses portfolio returns and see if your recommended portfolio (from an emotional risk point of view) is large enough to cover the lifestyle income wants important to you. If this is the right portfolio from both an emotional risk point of view and from an economic point of view, you know that you have enough money to retire.

The problem that many retirees face is lack of investment capital to fund their income needs and wants. To meet their income needs and wants they may knowingly, or unknowingly, take on considerable risk in their investment portfolios. It is not until the markets decline for a period of time, or one or more investments go sour, that the investor recognizes the amount of risk in their portfolio.

It is important to reassess the true value of all of your income needs and wants in relation to those things that are most important to you in your life. It is also critical that you ensure you are gaining all of the tax credits and benefits available to you as discussed in Chapter 6. Then you can redefine your income goals for your investments. These are very important steps that will help you avoid rolling the dice in your investment portfolio hoping (while worrying) that everything will work out in end. Remember, hope is not an investment strategy.

The Economy?

A third way to measure if now is the right time to retire is to look at the economy. The economy moves in cycles, from recessions to peaks and then back again. These cycles typically occur in 7 to 10 year periods. For those who retire at the end of a recession, the odds of running out of money in retirement are small. However, for those who retire at the beginning of a recession, the odds of running out of money can be quite high.

Your body, mind or health may be telling you that today is the day to retire. If there is a downturn in the economy, and if this is the day, you will need to be particularly prudent and cautious. Relying on your portfolio to produce the vast majority of income may prove to be a serious mistake. If you combine a higher risk portfolio with a market downturn, it is possible that your investments may suffer a sizeable loss and may never recover.

The best approach is to strive to have a low degree of risk at a modest level of income. If this isn't possible you may need to consider the purchase of an annuity for greater security, reduce expenses, work part time to supplement your income or postpone your retirement date.

The Importance of Portfolio Reviews

The last point about taming risk in your portfolio is to review your portfolio regularly from a pessimistic, moderate and optimistic perspective. A range of outcomes is always a wise consideration so as to keep your expectations at appropriate levels and to prepare for the unexpected. Every three to four months project your returns over the next 3, 6, 9 and 12 months based on different scenarios. Calculate the impact of a return in the low 17% return zone (the Red Zone = the pessimistic view). Then, calculate the impact of a return in the typical 66% return zone (the moderate return). If markets and the economy are doing well, project the outcome of above average growth (the optimistic outcome). This exercise will help you understand the impact of different scenarios on your portfolio and your level of comfort with the risk you are currently taking. You may want to complete this exercise with your advisor.

If you do not do this, odds are you may be lulled into a false sense of security that the investments you own are of low risk when in fact that may not be the case.

IN SUMMARY

Some of the advice in this chapter may seem contrary to advice you have heard about long term investing. This advice is the case because you are now drawing an income from your portfolio and the risks may be much greater for capital loss. Because of these higher risks, it is important to keep your basic needs and lifestyle wants in check which is why the "lifestyle planning" and "tax return management" components of the retirement plan are so critically important.

You may rely on your portfolio to give you an unlimited access to the fruits of success, but by doing so you may find that you are frequently disappointed with the results. This could be because of under-performance of both the portfolio and the markets overall, unexpected capital losses or unrealistic expectations on your part.

You must tame the risk and return of your portfolio. To do so at the highest level of efficiency, do this in conjunction with the other aspects of your overall retirement plan.

THINGS YOU NEED TO KNOW

- Investment portfolios have risk; perhaps more than what you may be aware.

- For every percentage of additional return you desire, you will increase the level of risk threefold. Risk and return is not a one to one relationship.

- Ideally you want to have a low risk, conservative portfolio in retirement earning a 5% to 7% annual rate of return.

- You may never have as much money in your portfolio as you do today. Liquidity, tax efficiency, low fees and a reasonable investment return are the four key consideration of an investment.

QUESTIONS YOU NEED TO ASK

- How much risk are you comfortable with at this stage in your life?
- What percent of your income do you wish to have come from variable sources?
- Where are we in the economic cycle? Is the economy in recession? When is a recovery expected to start?
- How low could your portfolio go before you begin to feel uncomfortable?
- How liquid are your investments?
- What are the total fees of your investments and is there a way to reduce these costs?
- Am I chasing returns? Does the return in the portfolio demonstrate risk?

THINGS YOU NEED TO DO

- Evaluate the risk profile of your portfolio on a regular basis.
- Evaluate your comfort with risk on a regular basis.
- Evaluate the risk profile of the market on a regular basis.
- Evaluate how much risk you really need to take in your portfolio on a regular basis.

DECISIONS YOU NEED TO MAKE

- To what extent are you prepared to be actively involved in your portfolio? This does not mean that you would have to "do it yourself" but rather be involved and take an active interest with your advisor.
- To what extent would you prefer to implement the 100% guaranteed solution and avoid all of the ups and downs of the market?

MASTER YOUR RETIREMENT
Taming the Risk and Return
of Your Investment Portfolio

TIPS

- Different advisors have different biases when it comes to risk, portfolio design and product selection. To help get the two of you on the same page, complete the same risk profile questionnaire so that you can compare your results.
- Do you and your advisor value the same investment traits regarding liquidity, fees, tax efficiency and yield? Have this discussion with your advisor.
- Always keep your eyes open for better investment products.

TRAPS

- Don't chase yield.
- Never be complacent about your portfolio or the market.
- Don't be seduced by investment products that appear to offer higher guarantees with fewer risks. Odds are that you may have to sacrifice liquidity or pay higher fees or be exposed to risks that you may not realize until it's too late.

CHAPTER 8

When Illness Strikes

Outstanding people have one thing in common: an absolute sense of mission.
ZIG ZIGLAR

Lawrence and Linda are 75 years old. While they are both very healthy and active themselves, not a month goes by where they don't hear about someone they know falling ill or battling with some form of health ailment. This is a common conversation among their peers.

They are doing everything they can to remain active, eat well, take vitamin supplements and see their physician regularly. Yet, they want to make sure that they are prepared in advance for a day when one of them may fall ill.

They are unsure of the full impact of an illness. What if the person who falls ill is the one who normally pays the bills and looks after the finances? How will they adapt?

What if the person who falls ill needs to receive long term care or move into a long term care facility? How will this impact their income and lifestyle?

Will they have enough income to support their medical needs? What other sources of income could they draw from?

Lawrence and Linda want to make sure they are ready for when an illness strikes. But they are unsure of what to do and how to go about doing it.

THE ISSUES

Recent statistics suggest that older Canadians in general are living healthy lives in their later years. However, age-related restrictions to life activities affect one in five seniors age 65 to 74, just under one in three between 75 and 85 and one half of seniors aged 85 or more.[1]

While there has been a noticeable decline in mortality from heart disease and strokes, cancer and respiratory diseases have increased. In addition, while women live longer than men, approximately two thirds of these extra years are spent living with a disability.

The vast majority of seniors take medication, stay in hospital longer and require the services of care giving (either informal or formal) for some portion of their later years.

The number one issue related to aging is the cost of long term care. Long term care facilities charge as much as $70 per day. Though the cost of long term care is subsidized by provincial governments, the resident is responsible for a portion of the cost. The long term care fee charged by the government is dependent upon the total gross income for both spouses. On the one hand you may feel that $70 per day is quite inexpensive given the treatment, meals and services provided. Yet, $70 per day is also equal to $25,550 for the year. The number one issue and risk to a couple in retirement is the ability to fund this expense while also maintaining the current home and lifestyle of the healthy spouse. In effect, when illness strikes, you may be funding the cost of two homes at the same time. The average length of stay in a long term care facility is three to five years. This could be a considerable expense for most families.

---

[1] Canada's Aging Population 2002, Health Canada

THE SOLUTIONS

You may find yourself in one of two different health related situations:

- **The need for treatment:** if you have just had a heart attack, stroke and or been diagnosed with cancer and need immediate treatment, or
- **The need for long term care:** when you require assistance with daily living over a longer period of time.

In each of these situations there is a need for diagnosis, treatment and cash. Some of the cash may come from your investments, assets or insurance while some may come from your tax return. Each of these options is described below.

In addition to this, there also needs to be clear instructions to those around you of how you wish your affairs to be handled. This is the legal aspect of handling an illness. At the end of the chapter we discuss briefly the importance of having a Will, a Power of Attorney and a Living Will.

Finally, to prepare for such a situation, some steps will be outlined at the end of this chapter to help you measure the impact of such an illness or long term care need.

THE NEED FOR TREATMENT

There are several important financial issues to be aware of as it relates to treatment.

Costs of Treatment

In Canada, most of the costs related to treatment will be paid for by the Provincial Government. However, you may find that the waiting time for treatment may be too long for your personal preference. In this instance you may wish to receive treatment outside of Canada. The cost of such treatment may range from $20,000 to $200,000. The cost for on-going medication may be as much as $2,000 per month and the cost for home renovations or the purchase of necessary medical equipment at home may also be significant.

Funding Options

There are several ways in which you can plan for these expenses in advance:

Critical Illness Insurance

Critical Illness Insurance is designed to pay you a lump sum, tax-free benefit in the event you are diagnosed with a critical illness and you survive for a period of 30 days after the diagnosis. The most common critical illnesses relate to a heart attack, stroke and cancer. The amount of benefit you receive is based on the amount you choose at the time of application. However, many group insurance programs now provide a basic flat amount of coverage as part of the overall group program. If you must choose the amount of coverage, choose an amount that is equal to approximately one year of before tax income. Critical illness insurance may allow you to seek the most appropriate treatment, in a timely manner and at the most appropriate location. The insurance is best purchased when you are younger as the cost of the premiums increase with age. Typically, coverage is available up to the age of 75.

International Health Insurance

Some health insurance products currently available in Canada provide funding for medical treatments abroad. The funding will also cover transportation and hotel costs for family. This type of coverage is ideal for busy entrepreneurs, executives and their families.

Investments

You can cash in some of your investments to pay for this treatment. Remember, if you cash in your RRSP investments you may find that your total taxable income now violates the "OAS Clawback Zone" which means you will pay a considerable amount of tax and clawback to fund this need and you will likely place a substantial dent in your RRSP portfolio.

Cashing in some of your non-registered investments will also deplete this source of capital and may eliminate its ability to generate future income. Cashing in your investments is an option, but it is less than ideal.

Taking a Loan

You can borrow money to pay for medical needs or complete home adaptations now needed as a result of the illness. This can be a good approach to protect your investment capital. The loan can be rolled into your mortgage so that you can pay it off over a long period of time. Many provinces provide grants and/or low-interest loans to cover the cost of home adaptations. Converting a portion of your investments into an annuity will enable you to receive a higher monthly income that is guaranteed for life. The higher income can help to make the monthly loan payment.

Tax Benefits

There are several tax benefits available to you when medical treatment is required including home renovation costs, moving expenses related to a move to a more accessible dwelling, expenses related to travel to receive medical service and expenses paid for medical benefits.

THE NEED FOR LONG TERM CARE

A significant financial risk to every family happens when one spouse enters a care facility while the other stays at home. Now you are covering the cost of two homes. If this happens early in retirement, 10 or more years of home or facility care expenses can place considerable financial hardship on the healthy spouse. It is important for the retired couple to understand these risks and to consider the burden and stress it can place on the entire family. The extended family will need to consider ways in which they can support the couple while the aging couple may wish to set out their instructions in advance to give guidance on these challenging and highly emotional issues.

Long Term Care Funding Options

Long Term Care Insurance

This type of insurance provides a monthly tax-free income of your choosing at the time of application. When you purchase long term care insurance you are purchasing a specific "daily" amount of benefit. For example, you may wish to consider $50, $75, $100, $200 or more of daily benefit. The plan is best purchased before you retire. The benefits are payable for a certain period of time or for life. When choosing long term care insurance you can opt for home care, facility care or both types of coverage. As you can see from the example at the beginning of the chapter, an additional $75 per day would be extremely beneficial to cover those long term costs.

The cost of long term care insurance is reasonably expensive and it is difficult to know if you should insure both spouses or just one. Insuring both spouses with long term care coverage is beneficial but expensive. If you were to insure only the husband, the healthy wife is now guaranteed to have enough money to continue to stay in her current home. Alternatively, if you were to insure only the wife, this may provide the wife, who is expected to outlive the husband in most cases, with long term financial security.

Some insurance companies are beginning to offer "first to claim" coverage whereby both spouses are part of the plan, but the benefit is paid to only the first individual who claims. This is an excellent product choice because you are covering the risk of both spouses yet only paying for one. In fact, the actual premium works out to be 10% to 15% less than the cost of two individual plans.

As with most forms of insurance, you are insuring the risk of incurring significant financial hardship. However, you never know if this is something that will impact you or not. The money may be really well spent or you may find that you never claim on this product and thus do not feel that you have received good value for your money invested into this product.

In some instances, if you do not make a long term care claim, some portion of your premiums paid can come back to you as a "return of premium" benefit.

Joint Last Survivor Insurance

A flexible long term solution is a Joint Last Survivor Insurance Policy, as you are guaranteed to eventually receive the insurance payout. The death benefit is paid on the last death.

The premiums on this type of life insurance are substantially less than individual life insurance coverage.

There are several benefits to this approach.

- Death benefit proceeds can be set up to by-pass your estate and go directly to your beneficiaries. The money received by your beneficiaries is then tax-free.
- You always know how much life insurance will be payable to your beneficiaries.
- If you know that your heirs are to receive this Joint Last Survivor life insurance benefit, then you may feel more comfortable drawing income from your investments, knowing you are still leaving a substantial legacy for your heirs.

Impaired Annuity

An annuity is identical to a pension plan. A lump sum of money is given to an insurance company which in turn guarantees to pay a monthly income for life. An "impaired" annuity provides a higher level of monthly income due to "less than standard health". If, due to your current health, your life expectancy is shorter than normal, the insurance company will take this into account when calculating the amount of monthly benefit provided to you. In the event that one spouse enters a long term care facility and there is a need to generate more income from investments, an impaired annuity may be an excellent solution for lifetime, guaranteed income.

Involuntary Separation

An "involuntary separation" occurs when one spouse enters a long term care facility, this move was not a choice, but a necessity. When this occurs, the other spouse can apply to have any income tested benefits calculated on a single income basis. Declaring an involuntary separation could lessen the amount of the OAS clawback. Talk with your tax professional to find the best solution for your situation. For more information on involuntary separation, contact your local Service Canada office.

Long Term Care Related Tax Benefits

There are several important tax credits in which you should be aware:

Caregiver Tax Credit

If you support and live with an infirm dependant in a home which you maintain, you may claim a specified amount for that dependant as a non-refundable credit against taxes payable.

To qualify, the dependant must meet these three criteria: a) be at least 18 years old, b) be either the child or grandchild of the taxpayer or the taxpayer's spouse or common-law partner, or the parent, grandparent, brother, sister, uncle, aunt, niece or nephew of the taxpayer or the taxpayer's spouse or common-law partner and resident in Canada at any time in the year, and c) be either the taxpayer's parent or grandparent and at least 65 years old or dependent on the taxpayer because of mental or physical infirmity

The Caregiver amount is $4,095 in 2008, and begins to be clawed back when the dependant's income reaches approximately $14,000 and is fully clawed back at $19,000 of income.

Infirm Adult Tax Credit

If you support a dependant who is at least 18 years of age and dependent on you because of mental or physical infirmity, you may claim a non-refundable credit against taxes payable. To qualify, the dependant must be your child or grandchild (or child or grandchild of your spouse or common-law partner, or the parent, grandparent, brother, sister, uncle, aunt, niece or nephew of the taxpayer or the taxpayer's spouse or common-law partner and resident in Canada at any time in the year). Note that you cannot claim both the Caregiver Credit and the Infirm Adult Credit at the same time.

The Infirm Adult Tax Credit is $4,095 in 2008. It begins to be clawed back at when the dependent's income reaches approximately $5,500 and is fully clawed back when income exceeds $10,000.

YOUR LEGAL AFFAIRS

Three important steps should be considered in regard to your personal affairs. Is your will up to date? Do you have a Power of Attorney? Have you completed a Living Will (health care directive)?

Last Will and Testament

This legal document tells the world who is going to look after your affairs after you die, and to whom your assets are to flow. This can be a very simple document or it can be extremely complex, depending on your personal situation. It is recommended you see a lawyer to prepare your will to ensure your requests will be carried out as you intended.

Power of Attorney

This document states the name, obligations and responsibilities of the person who will look after your affairs in the event you are not able to do so for yourself. Typically, this is a situation where you are unable to pay your own bills, look after your own investments or make your own financial decisions due to incapacity or illness.

The Living Will (Health Care Directive)

This document describes your wishes regarding the type of treatment you are to receive in the event that you may be suffering from a long illness, in great pain and are unlikely to recover. This is a very helpful document to your family, letting them know in advance your wishes in the event that such a situation may arise. This document can alleviate the need for caregivers and/or family members to struggle with difficult decisions during a time of extreme stress. The instructions on a Living Will should be clear and easily understood by medical personnel, it is recommended you speak with your doctor before you complete your Living Will.

IN SUMMARY

To assess your ability to survive an unexpected illness or long term care need, consider the following:

THINGS YOU NEED TO KNOW

- Both a short term illness and a long term care need can be a substantial expense.
- Specific insurance products can be purchased to pay for medical expenses.
- Tax deductions and tax credits may be available to offset the cost of medical expenses.
- A substantial financial risk you face is the need for long term care assistance for a long period of time, while the healthy spouse lives in your current home. The cost of financing two "homes" can be considerable.

QUESTIONS YOU NEED TO ASK

- What is the financial risk to you?
- What sources of capital could you draw on to cover these expenses?
- Is there a shortfall? Would you feel more comfortable having part of the risk insured?
- Are you claiming all available expenses and credits?
- How will an illness impact the healthy spouse? Will the healthy spouse require assistance with the finances?

THINGS YOU NEED TO DO

- Update your Will.
- Prepare a Power of Attorney and Living Will.
- Discuss the Will, Power of Attorney and Living Will with your children so that everyone is aware of your wishes.
- Prepare a financial analysis noting the impact to the healthy spouse in the event the other spouse enters a long term care facility.
- Decide if you would feel more comfortable with the purchase of long term care insurance.

MASTER YOUR RETIREMENT
When Illness Strikes

TIPS

- Be prepared. Formulate a health care plan and put it in writing so your family can follow your wishes. Review this plan every one to three years.
- Discuss your health care plan with your family members so that everyone is aware of the game plan.
- Consider purchasing insurance to offset the cost of long term care.

TRAPS

- Never assume that it will not happen to you.
- One or two unfortunate medical circumstances (and the corresponding medical expenses) may erase a lifetime of prudent financial decisions. Do not underestimate the risks and the costs.
- Don't assume that the government will always pay for these expenses. As our population ages the government has no choice but to charge more for these services to the people who are using them. The government will need to charge more because at some point in time in the future there is expected to be more people retired than working.

CHAPTER 9

Being on Your Own

Paint a masterpiece daily. Always autograph your work with excellence.
GREG HICKMAN

Theresa and Don held hands waiting for Dr. Smith to give them the results of the tests. Don had been receiving cancer treatments for two years now, but he was growing weaker and weaker as time wore on. Don had been in the hospital now for almost six months. Unfortunately, the news was not good and there was nothing more the doctors could do for Don. It was just a matter of time.

Don is 75 and Theresa is 74. Both had been quite active up until two years ago when the first diagnosis was made. They both remained focused on Don's health, never daring to think that he may pass away before his time. But now it was a different story, the unthinkable was about to happen.

As the shock of the news set in for Theresa, a greater fear also took over her thoughts. She didn't know very much about their household finances, his pension, their investments or their taxes. Don had always taken care of their finances. All of their children were grown, married and living in other provinces. Who should she talk to? Who could she count on for help? Would she have enough money? How would she spend her time? What would she do?

Not only was she devastated to lose her lifelong partner, but she was also sad about the unfulfilled dreams they shared together. They had so many plans that now would never come to pass. She was also terrified of making the wrong decision regarding their finances. Theresa was really scared.

THE ISSUES

There are many important financial issues that arise when one spouse survives the other:

- How much income will you have after your spouse passes away?
- What are your new monthly expenses?
- Will you have enough income to live on?
- Is this income safe and secure?
- Where is the cheque book, the bank accounts and the tax forms?
- When do you file the tax returns and who looks after this?
- Who is looking after your investments?
- Where are the Wills?
- Do you have enough money to pay for a proper funeral?

There are also many important softer issues that arise. Many of these will depend on the age of the surviving spouse:

- How will you spend your time?
- Who will you spend your time with?
- Who can you talk to about your grief and sadness?
- What should you do with the cottage?
- What should you do with the family home?
- What do you need to do to feel safe?

While the questions may appear to be complex, the answers are quite simple. You need to take a deep breath, gain control, tie up loose ends and then begin to plan ahead for the future.

THE SOLUTIONS

After the funeral, the surviving spouse can often be faced with a tidal wave of issues, questions and decisions. At a time when you may wish to just sit back, reflect, remember and grieve in the quiet and comfort of your own home, many important issues need to be discussed. It is also possible that the surviving spouse is meeting his/her advisors for the first time, or for the first time in many years.

The best approach is to identify the priorities and do a few things at a time. Each of these priorities can be broken down into three distinct areas: gain control, tie up loose ends and plan for the future.

GAIN CONTROL

Great comfort and peace of mind will come from a basic understanding of where you stand financially. To gain control means that you have control over your bank accounts, your expenses and your income and you have an understanding of where they are, how much they are and the amount of money you have to spend each month.

If your bank accounts are "jointly held" between both spouses, there are no issues of concern. You can continue to write cheques and pay bills from this account. However, if one or more accounts were in the name of the deceased spouse, these accounts must be identified and transferred to an account in the name of the surviving spouse. To do this, speak to your local bank branch, they will help you with this process.

To avoid difficult situations with bank accounts, ensure that all accounts are jointly held with rights of survivorship.

Make a list of your monthly expenses. Look at the last two to three months of bank statements to see which expenses are automatically drawn from your account and which expenses had been paid for by cheque or credit card each month. Many people keep excellent records in their cheque book and this can be another great place to look when sizing up the monthly expenses. Watch the incoming mail very closely for overdue notices of payment. By paying close attention to the incoming mail you will begin to gain an understanding of your monthly expenses.

Now that you are on your own, it is important to identify your income sources and any changes to that income as a result of the loss of your partner.

Canada Pension Plan

Prior to Don's death, he was receiving a Canada Pension Plan (CPP) monthly income benefit. After his death, the surviving spouse will no longer receive this income. Instead, in its place, will be a survivor's monthly income benefit. In general, the total maximum amount that the surviving spouse will receive from the Canada Pension Plan is equal to the maximum monthly income benefit available at that time. In 2008 the maximum income benefit was $884.58 per month and the survivor pension amount (after age 65) is $530.75. If the surviving spouse is already receiving a monthly benefit of $600 per month, for example, they will receive the maximum of $884.58 rather than the combined amount ($600 + $530.75 = $1130.75). If the surviving spouse is already receiving $200 per month in CPP benefits, they will receive the full $530.75 in survivor benefit since the sum of the two is less than the maximum of $884.58.

For most surviving spouses, this will mean that the total CPP monthly income benefit will likely decrease.

You must notify the Canada Pension Plan of the death of your spouse through one of the Service Canada offices in your area. When you do, you will also complete an application for a "Lump Sum Death Benefit" that will pay you a one time payment of $2,500 (2008).

Old Age Security

Prior to Don's passing, both he and Theresa were each receiving approximately $500 per month in Old Age Security (OAS) income. As of Don's death his OAS benefit will end resulting in a loss of $6,000 in annual before-tax income.

Employer Pension Plan

If Don had a pension plan with a previous employer(s), the monthly income benefit on this plan may be reduced by approximately 33% to 50%. You must notify the employer of the passing of your spouse. They will advise you of the amount of pension income that you will receive from this point forward.

Annuity Income

An annuity is similar to a pension plan and may also be reduced by as much as 33% to 50%. Notify the insurance company of the passing of your spouse and they will notify you of the amount of annuity income you will receive from this point forward.

RRIF and Other Investments

As with the bank accounts, you must convert the ownership of these investments to the name of the surviving spouse. In many instances you can combine the RRIFs together and have one or two large accounts rather than several small accounts. Your investment advisor or a representative from each company can provide you with the necessary documents to complete these changes.

In many instances these accounts will be jointly owned with rights of survivorship. This means that the account will continue on as is without any difficulties. You will, however, need to change the ownership of the investment to the surviving spouse in due course.

NOTE: In January of each year you will receive an annual investment statement from any company holding your investments. Watch your mail closely during this time to make sure you haven't missed changing over any of your investments.

Life Insurance Proceeds

It is a top priority to apply for any life insurance proceeds that are payable to you. Contact your insurance advisor to assist you with this or speak directly with the insurance company. In most cases, they will need a copy of the funeral director's death certificate to process the claim.

NOTE: There may be life insurance protection on your loans, mortgages and even your credit cards. It is important to apply for all such payments.

By taking control over your bank accounts, your income and your expenses, you now have control over your personal finances. You will begin to see whether you have enough income to cover your monthly expenses.

At this stage, you have gained control over your financial affairs, but not made any significant changes or decisions. Before making any decisions, you will need to probate the Will of the deceased spouse. Probating the Will is done with the assistance of a lawyer. Probating a Will is the formal process to ensure the Last Will and Testament of a deceased individual is fulfilled according to the terms and conditions of the Will and the local provincial court certifies the process. This may take several weeks or months to complete. Once the court has approved the probated Will the financial institutions may require a copy for their records to proceed with changing the ownership of the RRIF and other investment assets to the name of the surviving spouse.

Some financial institutions will proceed with changing the ownership of the investments from one spouse to another if they are provided a copy of the death certificate and the beneficiaries all sign a form that releases the financial institution from any liability. Contact your financial institution to check on the documents required.

There are ways to prepare for this situation in advance and relieve the stress for the surviving spouse:

- Convert your assets (home, non-registered investment account and bank accounts) to joint ownership today.
- Know in advance the changes that will occur to pension plans and annuities on the death of either spouse.
- Prepare a monthly budget and share it with your spouse.

- Prepare a list of all bank and investment accounts.
- Prepare a list of advisors and who should be contacted for each area of knowledge.
- Tell your spouse and Executor the location of your Will.
- Discuss these implications with your children so that everyone knows the overall game plan.

Unfortunately, some adult children prey on the lone surviving parent to help them through a financial crisis or to support them in their next business endeavour. In many cases, a surviving spouse may feel lonely and vulnerable and can be easily manipulated or pushed to lend or give money to this child. The other siblings may not be aware of what is happening until they realize their brother or sister has depleted a large portion of their father/mother's investment capital. Not only will this impact the surviving spouse's standard of living, but has also impacted the inheritance for the others—then the sparks really begin to fly.

To avoid such a situation, some or all of the assets could be left to the surviving spouse in a "Spousal Trust". By doing so the surviving spouse would receive income from the trust but no capital could be withdrawn (unless specifically provided for in the trust deed).

If you, as the surviving spouse, feel uncomfortable or threatened by a family member asking you for a loan or gift of money, tell someone. Tell other family members, friends or a professional such as a bank employee, social worker or law enforcement professional. Remember, you are not only protecting your income, but also the legacy you will leave to your family/or and community.

TIE UP LOOSE ENDS

There are many financial issues that need to be dealt with, but not all are necessarily urgent and can wait until you have completed the first steps discussed previously.

Real Estate Ownership

The ownership of your real estate must be changed to the name of the surviving spouse. This includes your home, your cottage, vacation home and any other properties. If the property is jointly owned you will remain an owner of the property and have rights to make decisions about the property. However, for greater clarity you will want to change the ownership to the name of the surviving spouse within a reasonable period of time.

Cars

Do you need to insure and operate two cars? Does it make sense to sell one car and thus stop the monthly insurance payment? The sooner you do this the better, but this is not an urgent issue.

Credit Cards

Cancel all credit cards in the name of the deceased spouse. But before you do so, check to see if there is any life insurance or accidental death insurance coverage on any outstanding balance.

Memberships

Cancel the annual membership to various clubs that the deceased spouse enjoyed on their own. If you also attend the same club, you may not need to make any changes until it is time to renew the memberships.

Subscriptions

Cancel magazine or other subscriptions that do not interest you.

Medical Insurance

Cancel coverage for deceased spouse.

PLAN FOR YOUR FUTURE

Planning for the future may not take place for a year or even two years after the death of the spouse. Of course, the sooner it is done the better, but the surviving spouse may not be ready to take these steps until they have had a chance to work through their grief. Making big decisions while grieving can be extremely stressful and may result in feelings of making the wrong decision because you felt rushed or confused. It is always best to let things settle down first before taking on significant decisions.

It is now time to review your retirement vision and your retirement income plan. You have experienced a significant life changing event which will affect your plans for the future. Follow the processes described in the first chapters of this book and revisit your plan every three to five years.

Assess Your Taxes

As discussed in the previous chapters, you need to know if your income is moving into higher tax brackets or higher clawback levels. If your income is entering these levels consider ways to reduce your total taxable income. When considering how to do this, the first step will be to review your income and expenses.

IN SUMMARY

This book is about Mastering Your Retirement. To Master Your Retirement we recognize that there are several phases that you will go through throughout your retirement years. If we know in advance what these phases will look like, we can do some very important pro-active planning. It is clear that one day one spouse will be gone and one will survive. If the surviving spouse knows about all the important issues in advance it can make life, at this most difficult time, as calm and assured as possible.

While your children were young, you often encouraged to "clean up their mess". The same is true for adults. One such "mess" relates to your investments, real estate, Wills, and finances. If you "clean up the mess" for your surviving spouse and he/she will continue on with life without encountering financial obstacles or surprises.

THINGS YOU NEED TO KNOW

- When one spouse passes away, your household income may decrease.
- The deceased's OAS benefit will stop.
- CPP may be reduced.
- Annuity income or pension plan income may also be reduced.
- Know in advance how the death of a spouse will affect the financial picture of the survivor.

QUESTIONS YOU NEED TO ASK

- Which assets are jointly owned and which assets are not jointly owned?

- Are the assets that are jointly owned referred to as "tenants in common" or "joint tenants with rights of survivorship"? These two descriptions mean two different things. The latter option is the most preferred.

- Are all bank accounts, investment accounts and insurance policies listed in one location?

- Where is the Will?

- Is there a list of all advisors and their roles?

THINGS YOU NEED TO DO

- Take a moment to "analyze" the financial future of the surviving spouse. To do so, assume that one spouse has passed away and the surviving spouse is on their own. What decisions will they have to make? What information will they need?

- Plan your funeral arrangements in advance.

- Discuss and share your plans with your children so that everyone knows the game plan.

- If there is a risk of the surviving spouse being taken advantage of by an unscrupulous family member(s), consider putting most or all assets into a "Spousal Trust".

MASTER YOUR RETIREMENT
Being on Your Own

TIPS

- Take the time to make sure both you and your spouse know and trust your advisors.
- Review your retirement plan every two to four years, taking into account the five different phases that you will go through in retirement.
- Communicate your plans to other family members so that everyone is on the same page and are able to help the surviving spouse in a consistent manner.
- Consider the outcome for the surviving spouse when you decide which pension option to take at retirement.

TRAPS

- Be careful not to give away too much money too soon. When planning to give an inheritance early, consider this decision thoroughly and clearly. Be wary of family members who try to influence your decisions.
- Don't avoid discussing the inevitable; doing so may leave the surviving spouse in dire straights.

CHAPTER 10

Choose Your Beneficiaries Wisely... Don't Leave It to the Taxman

When it's all over, it's not who you were. It's whether you made a difference.
BOB DOLE

A week after the funeral, the family gathered to read Mary's last Will and Testament. Mary had lived a long and gracious life, given back to her community in many ways and played an active role in the lives of her children and grandchildren. While the family was naturally sad, they also admired the life that Mary and her husband Bill had lived. But what really impressed the family the most was the lasting legacy they left behind. Bill, Mary's husband, had passed away a year earlier.

Mary's total estate value was just over $2 million. This was very significant for the modest life and income that she and Bill had throughout their life together. It was also amazing to see that much of this money will be going to the beneficiaries tax-free.

The family knew that considerable planning had always taken place and both their father and their mother wanted to make sure that the taxes were minimized in their estate. Each family member would receive a significant inheritance while also giving a generous amount of money to charity.

Bill and Mary always enjoyed their life, and the decisions they made along the way were highly influenced by their legacy desires. They both felt very strongly about leaving this world a better place in some small way—and they did.

THE ISSUES

How do you find the right balance between meeting today's income needs while planning for tax efficiency and greater estate benefits down the road?

The answer to this question is "good planning". You need to know which assets will generate tax in your estate and which assets will not. Your objective is to gravitate towards the tax-free assets and move away from those that are less tax efficient.

What can you do to enhance your legacy to your family and community? What can you do to leave the world a better place?

This can be achieved in several ways, many of which are not necessarily financially related. Your legacy may be your time and commitment to a particular cause in the community. Perhaps you are already planning on leaving a financial donation to this cause. To multiply your legacy you may wish to consider the use of life insurance.

Have you chosen your beneficiaries wisely? In many cases the tax department is the largest single beneficiary of your estate. The estate could pay 30% to 40% of the value of the estate in taxes unless a) you are able to accumulate more tax-free assets or b) pay the taxes that are due with fewer dollars. Are you aware of all you can do to make this happen? After all, why wouldn't you want to do this? Why would you purposely leave more money to the government than any other beneficiary?

When planning your legacy you want to make sure you "begin with the end in mind". By planning ahead and focusing on the final outcomes you can make sure you make appropriate decisions along the way.

Now let's take a look at how Bill and Mary's story evolved.

THE SOLUTIONS

Bill and Mary's family home was valued at $500,000. The home is tax-free because the house was classified as their principal residence under the Income Tax Act. Bill and Mary also purchased a joint last survivor life insurance policy for $1 million close to 15 years ago; the proceeds of this policy are passed on to the heirs tax-free. The remaining value is the investment portfolio. Much of this value was held in the Tax-Free Savings Account they opened in 2009. Over the past 15 years they have diligently deposited the maximum of $10,000 ($5,000 per person) a year into this plan. The principal investment as well as the interest on this investment money is received tax-free into the estate.

Fifteen years ago Bill and Mary found a way to multiply the value of their estate. They were planning all along to leave $200,000 of their estate to charity. However, they found that they could now use this same $200,000 to purchase a $1 million life insurance policy and triple the value of their legacy. They decided to leave $100,000 to six different charitable organizations that included helping the poor, medical research, education grants and their church.

Bill and Mary also decided to leave $600,000 to each of their two children in the form of a testamentary trust. The testamentary trust is taxed similar to an individual tax payer. This will help save thousands of dollars in tax over the remaining life of their children as well as their grandchildren.

If Bill and Mary had done nothing to plan for their final transition, their estate would be subject to several hundred thousand dollars in additional taxes and they would have had less money to share. Bill and Mary were able to triple the amount of money they would give to charity as well as double the amount of money they would give to their children and grandchildren.

Bill and Mary's lasting legacy was substantial:

- Additional income and financial resources for their children.
- Additional resources for important community projects and charities for today and years to come.

- The memories and laughter they shared throughout their life with their children and grandchildren.
- Over the past 10 years Bill and Mary collaborated in writing a book about their lives, their family history, the lessons they learned and the wisdom they gained. This book was presented to the family at the time the Will was read.

ENHANCING YOUR PERSONAL LEGACY

Peace of mind and happiness is derived from a sense of satisfaction, satisfaction of a job well done or a life well lived. Satisfaction comes from knowing that you took some risks along the way, you always did your best, your relationships were healthy and loving and, in some small way, the world is a better place today because of you.

Your legacy is not just a financial legacy. Your legacy may be your children and grandchildren, the volunteer work you've done in the community, the contributions you've made to make the community a better place, the time spent coaching other children and adults and the memories and the laughter shared.

What are the activities that give you the most satisfaction? How could you enhance your satisfaction?

- Would you set up a scholarship fund for your favorite academic pursuit?
- Would you volunteer to spend your time with children?
- Would you write a book describing your experiences when travelling abroad?
- Would you spend more time visiting with family and friends?
- Would you volunteer your time at the local food bank; would you deliver Meals on Wheels?
- Would you dedicate more time and energy to those in our society who are less fortunate?
- Would you spend more time learning something new?

- Would you spend time getting the work of others acknowledged? Perhaps there is someone you know who should be included in your local sports hall of fame?

There are so many things that one can do to enhance their personal legacy. Enhancing your personal legacy is about enhancing your personal sense of satisfaction and making the world a better place. What would you like to do today, to increase your sense of satisfaction and enhance the world around you? This is the heart and soul of your lasting legacy!

Take a moment now and start making a list of all the things that are important to you. How can you multiply the benefit or outcome of these things? With these thoughts in mind, what do you feel could be your lasting legacy?

HAVE YOU CHOSEN YOUR BENEFICIARIES WISELY?

Whether you like it or not, the tax department will be one of the beneficiaries of your estate. It is your choice where your money goes when you die. Do you want to do everything you can to minimize the tax payable?

Taxable Assets

- **RRIF/RRSP investments:** The remaining value of your **registered** investments will be fully taxable in the estate of the last surviving spouse. When the first spouse passes away registered investments can be transferred to the surviving spouse without any tax implications. However, when the second spouse dies, all remaining registered investments are taxable as income. For example, if there were $500,000 of RRIF investments at the time of death, the $500,000 would be taxed as income. In this case approximately 40% of the value would go to the tax department.

- **Non-registered investments:** These investments are deemed to be sold at the time of death. Any remaining capital gains will now be taxed. A capital gain is the difference between the current market value and the cost base of the investment account. The cost base is the amount of the original investment plus any interest or dividend income received minus any withdrawals. When the capital gain amount is determined, 50% of the gain is taxable at your marginal tax rate. For example, if the value of the remaining investment account is $500,000 and the cost base is determined to be $300,000, the capital gain is the difference between the two (in this case $200,000). 50% of the capital gain is taxable. 50% of $200,000 is $100,000. This amount is added to your income and taxed accordingly. Odds are that 40% or more would disappear in tax.

- **Real estate:** Your principal residence is tax-free whereas other forms of personal use real estate are not. A common example of this is the family cottage. The cottage would be taxed in a manner similar to other non-registered investments. The amount of tax to be paid is based on the deemed market value of the property at the time of death. The amount that is taxable is the difference between the deemed market value and the cost base of the property. The cost base is the amount paid for the cottage plus any additional costs for renovations and upgrades. The difference between the market value and the cost base is the capital gain. 50% of the capital gain is added to income in the estate. You can apply the Principal Residence Exemption to any property at this time, preferably the one with the largest capital gain. Remember also that U.S. real estate may attract additional estate taxes in the U.S.

- **Rental properties:** During their use rental properties will have been depreciated for tax write-off purposes. This depreciation may be recaptured for tax purposes depending on the market value at the time of death, meaning the total amount taxable is a combination of the capital gain plus the recaptured depreciation.

- **An incorporated business enterprise:** An incorporated business enterprise is taxed in the same way as real estate and is subject to Capital Gains Tax.

Non-Taxable Assets

- **The principal residence:** The gain in value on the property you declare as your principal residence is not taxed when sold. You can declare any home to be your principal residence but you can only claim one home as your principal residence at one time. In some instances, if your cottage value has risen more than your city home, you may wish to declare your cottage to be your principal residence. You do not have to declare your principal residence exemption until the time of sale or death.

- **Tax-Free Savings Account (TFSA):** The new Tax-Free Savings Account, launched in January 2009, can be very beneficial when planning your estate. The income, growth and capital gain value is all tax-free. The account enables you to invest up to $5,000 per year per spouse. If you do not invest the full $5,000 in any one year, you can carry over the difference to the following year. If you withdraw money from the TFSA you can put back the same amount in the future. In other words, you re-create the available contribution room when you make a withdrawal.

- **Life insurance proceeds:** Life insurance proceeds are tax-free. Proceeds which are named to specific beneficiaries go directly to them, tax-free, and not through the estate, where the funds would have been subject to probate.

To pay the least amount of tax in the estate, you should minimize the amount of registered investments at the time of death in favour of tax-free proceeds such as the ones just discussed.

TAX REDUCTION STRATEGIES

To reduce the tax in your estate, consider one or more of the following tax reduction strategies.

Charitable Giving

There is a great opportunity to reduce taxes through charitable giving. When completing the tax return for the estate, you can opt to make a charitable contribution up to 100% of the value of the year's taxable income. If, for example, the total taxable income in the estate is $200,000 then you could choose to give all of this income to charity. By doing so you are able to reduce taxes.

Another component of this strategy is to donate "publicly traded" securities to charities. This would eliminate the capital gains taxes on these securities while also creating a tax credit. To receive this benefit you must state in the Will that these securities are to be donated to a specific charity. Remember, however, that the total charitable gifts can be up to the total earned income in the year of death.

Use and Re-Create

Convert all RRIF income to an annuity, which acts like a pension plan. A lump sum of money is invested with an insurance company in return for a guaranteed lifetime income. Often the income received is greater than the RRIF income that was received before this conversion was made. In many situations most or all of the additional income received will go toward the funding of a new joint last survivor life insurance plan. The life insurance plan is paid to your beneficiaries on death. Because you have converted all of the RRIF assets to an annuity, when you die the annuity will end and nothing will go to your estate (unless you die within a guaranteed period that you selected at the time of purchase). This strategy uses all of the RRIF assets but then recreates these same assets for the beneficiaries. By following these steps you have a risk free lifetime income in retirement, no tax in the estate, plus a tax-free benefit paid to your heirs.

Life Insurance to Fund the Tax Bill

Another approach is to calculate in advance the expected tax bill in the estate and fund the tax bill with life insurance thus removing the burden from the heirs and leaving a larger legacy. Perhaps the tax bill is expected to be $300,000. You could purchase a joint last survivor life insurance plan for $300,000. The cost of the premium is dependent on your age, and you may be surprised at how low the cost will be. The insurance would be paid to the estate at the exact same time as the tax bill was due. This is another way you can minimize the effect of the tax bill on the estate, assuming the tax bill is something that you cannot avoid. We refer to this as "paying the tax bill" with fewer dollars since the cost to fund the insurance is much less than saving up the same amount of money over time.

Testamentary Trusts

Once the tax bill is paid, you can pass on your assets to your heirs in a structure that could provide great tax benefits to them longer term. Let's assume that each grown adult child receives $600,000 of after-tax money inside of a testamentary trust. Income earned in the trust would be taxed on a marginal rate basis.

Let's assume that the beneficiary, who lives in Ontario, already earns an income of $50,000. The taxes paid would be approximately $9,707. If the beneficiary receives the inheritance personally, invests the money and then earns an additional $30,000 of interest income, the $80,000 of total income now pays taxes of $19,985. This means that the $30,000 of interest income creates $10,277 of tax.

By comparison, if this same interest income was taxed inside the testamentary trust, the tax due would be closer to $6,615. This means that by receiving the inheritance inside the testamentary trust the beneficiary avoids approximately $3,662 in tax each year. Over 20 years the total tax savings would exceed $73,000.

A testamentary trust is set up through the Will of the last survivor. The trust details can be flexible allowing all of the money in the trust to be drawn out if it was prudent to do so. Yet, by setting up the trust you have created a lifetime of tax savings on this money.

NOTE: By using a testamentary trust structure in your Will you are not reducing taxes in the estate. Rather you are reducing income taxes for your beneficiaries in the long term.

Topping Income Up to Bracket

In Canada we live under a marginal rate tax bracket system. As you reach certain levels of income the next dollar of income you earn will be taxed at a higher rate. In some instances it is beneficial to take additional RRSP/RRIF withdrawals up to the next tax bracket level and invest this money into an after-tax account (ideally the TFSA). By doing so you avoid having the remaining RRIF assets taxed at a higher rate on your estate tax return. This point emphasizes how important it is to manage your tax return year by year.

If you do not consider closely who your beneficiaries will be, odds are the tax department will sneak in and be your largest beneficiary. Significant tax savings can occur when a charitable contribution is made, when tax efficient investment vehicles are used, when you strategically use your principal residence exemption, and when you use life insurance to either expand your estate or to pay for the tax. Once the estate has been cleared, a testamentary trust can be used for the long term tax saving benefit of the beneficiaries.

Whatever you do, don't leave a blank cheque for the tax department. Choose your beneficiaries wisely.

BEGIN WITH THE END IN MIND

Steven Covey, in his best selling book "7 Habits of Highly Effective People", writes of the benefits of "beginning with the end in mind". What does this mean?

If we know what we wish to achieve then we can work backwards to see what is needed to achieve the outcome. This chapter has highlighted several suggestions to consider:

- Minimize taxable investments in your estate.
- Use life insurance to pay the tax on those investments that are taxable in the estate with a substantially smaller financial outlay.
- Use life insurance to create tax-free proceeds for the beneficiaries.
- Apply the principle residence exemption to the property with the greatest capital gain.
- Consider the use of testamentary trusts in your Will.
- Consider using charitable contributions to reduce taxes owing.

The Survivor Analysis

Completing this analysis will illustrate the impact, both financial and otherwise, of the death of spouse A on spouse B and vice versa. Ask these questions:

- What are the terms of the Will?
- If Dad passed away first, what will be the financial impact on Mom?
- How will her income change?
- Is this enough income?
- What are the tax implications?
- What decisions should she consider if she needed more income at that time?
- What is her guaranteed income expected to be at that time?
- Does her guaranteed income cover her basic income needs?
- How does this situation change if Mom passes away first?
- What are the directions in Mom's Will? Should the Will be changed due to a change in circumstances?
- Where are the risks?
- What are the opportunities?
- What are the tax implications?

The Final Estate Analysis

The final estate analysis focuses on the tax implications, charitable giving and estate transfer plan when both spouses are deceased.

- What directions and bequests are included in the Will?
- How much tax is to be paid?
- How much money is to be transferred to the beneficiaries of the estate and what will be the impact to the beneficiaries from a taxation point of view going forward? Remember, if the bequest will result in a high rate of tax, the time to reduce this tax is now. If you are considering setting up a testamentary trust to reduce the tax effects on your heirs, it must be provided for prior to death in the Will.
- Are there strong desires to leave money to specific charities? If so, what are the tax implications of charitable donations and where should these donations come from? (i.e.: should any charitable donations come from individual stocks so as to receive more favorable tax treatment than cash).

- Is there a way to enhance/increase the amount of the charitable contribution to reduce taxes payable and increase estate value for the benefit of the heirs?

- Is there a way to reduce taxes or pay fewer tax dollars through the use of life insurance?

- Are there specific assets that should go to specific individuals and why? Has this been communicated to all the stakeholders in the family?

- Do you wish to see your assets divided amongst your children in a particular way to avoid awkward family arguments?

- Who have you named as the Executor of your Will? Are all family members aware of this decision and are they comfortable with this? Your Will is often the last communication you have with your children, in many instances it is beneficial to have all children named as executors. One or two of the children may do the bulk of the work and some of the children may decide that they do not need to have signing authority after the fact, but naming them all as co-executors can be a step that will reduce family conflict.

One of the best ways to Master Your Retirement is to take the time to plan. Explore the risks and opportunities. Think ahead and "begin with the end in mind". Do this and you will Master the Final Outcome.

IN SUMMARY

THINGS YOU NEED TO KNOW

- Any remaining value in your RRSP or RRIF is fully taxable as income in the estate of the last survivor.
- Any remaining investment assets or real estate is subject to capital gains tax in the estate of the last survivor.
- The use of the Principal Residence Exemption eliminates the capital gain on that property. If the capital gain on the cottage is greater than the capital gain on your city home (over the same period of time), you may wish to apply your exemption to the cottage.
- The value of the Tax-Free Savings Account at the time of death is non-taxable.
- Insurance proceeds are non-taxable.
- You can contribute up to 100% of your earned income in the year of death to a charity.

QUESTIONS YOU NEED TO ASK

- At this moment, how much of your current estate would be taxable?
- How much tax would have been paid by the estate?
- Is there a way to reduce this tax?
- How much do you wish to give to charity?
- Is there a way to multiply this gift using life insurance?
- Is there an opportunity to withdraw additional RRIF assets (i.e.: topping up to bracket) to potentially reduce taxes owing in the estate down the road?

THINGS YOU NEED TO DO

- Create an estate optimization strategy for the next five years. The goal is to reduce potential taxes in the estate by taking certain steps today.

- Maximize annual contributions into the Tax-Free Savings Account.

- Keep track of the cost base of both the cottage and your city home. This will help to determine on which property to apply the Principal Residence Exemption.

- Consider the benefit of Joint Last Survivor life insurance as a way to "pay taxes with few dollars" or to multiply the value of your estate for charitable or other purposes.

MASTER YOUR RETIREMENT
Choose Your Beneficiaries Wisely...
Don't Leave It to the Taxman

TIPS

- The average life expectancy is 80, however, you may wish to project as far as age 90 to 95 due to the trend toward increasing longevity.
- The Will is your last chance to speak to your children. Make sure the language used treats them all fairly; one way to do this is to have all of your children as co-executors of the Will.
- A testamentary trust must be set up through your Will. It cannot be set up by the executors of your estate after you die.
- It's not what you have; it's how much you keep—after-tax, after-fees and after-inflation.

TRAPS

- Without pro-active planning, it is highly likely the tax department could be the largest single beneficiary in your estate. You have the opportunity to change this by planning a tax efficient estate strategy.
- Make sure that any planning you do to reduce taxes in your final estate does not negatively impact the surviving spouse while he/she is alive.

Conclusions

There's retirement...and then there's "Mastering Your Retirement".

To Master Your Retirement consider the facts, figures and information contained in this book. Seek the right balance between health, relationships and your wealth for both you and your spouse. Consider the importance of the following these ten steps:

1. **Always start with your vision.** Project your lifestyle vision and milestones for the next three to five years. Include all aspects of your life, your health and your relationships. Continue to update your vision every twelve to thirty-six months.

2. **Identify your income needs and wants.** Project your basic income needs for the next few years and match this up with guaranteed sources of income. Project your lifestyle income wants and match this up with your variable sources of income.

3. **Understand your changing financial risk profile.** Update your Financial Risk Profile and ensure that your current investment portfolio and lifestyle are always consistent with this profile. Be true to yourself and do not take any unnecessary risks.

4. **Balance the income and growth potential of your investment portfolio with your lifestyle vision and income needs.** Measure the income and growth potential of your current investment portfolio based on your risk profile and your income needs Are your income needs greater than the income you expect to receive from the portfolio? Will you need to take more risk to achieve your income benchmark? If these are not in balance you must make changes to either your income needs or the structure of your portfolio. Whatever you do, don't compromise on your risk profile (don't take more risk than what you are comfortable with).

5. **Manage your tax.** Measure the tax efficiency of your income for the current year and for the next three to five years. Make sure you are staying within the clawback zones and receiving as tax efficient an income as possible. Make modifications to your investment portfolio and other sources of income to meet your tax efficiency objectives.

6. **Measure your health care risks.** As you grow older, you or your spouse may need ongoing home care or facility care. Both options can be extremely expensive. If this happens in the next three to five years, what would you do and what would be the financial impact? Spend time to consider the possibilities and make informed decisions for the best future course of action.

7. **Measure the survivor risks.** Eventually, one of you will be on your own. What if this happens in the next three to five years? What would you do and what would be the financial impact? Spend time to consider these possibilities and make informed decisions as to the best future course of action.

8. **Measure the final outcome.** As you and your spouse end your life's journey, how will your final affairs be wound up and what will be the implications? Will family harmony be intact? Will taxes be minimized? What will be your lasting legacy?

9. **Take action.** Update your Will, Power of Attorney, Living Will, investment portfolio, and your life and health insurance as needed to meet your objectives.

10. **Communicate.** Share your plans and strategies with your family. Communicating your wishes clearly will decrease or completely avoid misunderstandings, family arguments and relieve the stress of wondering "What would Mom and Dad want me to do?"

By following these steps every three to five years and by paying attention to the five phases of retirement you will truly Master Your Retirement.

You will:

- adapt to changing circumstances easily,
- reap the benefits of tax efficiency,
- live the life you dreamed of,
- sleep comfortably knowing your portfolio has the correct amount of risk for you and your basic income needs will always be met,
- pro-actively plan your future,
- leave nothing to chance,
- avoid family conflicts and miscommunication,
- maximize your lasting legacy for generations to come.

Life is short, but also generous and bountiful. Every minute of every day is so very valuable. Hopefully the messages in this book have given you ideas to enhance and add joy, wonder and spice to your life.

All the best on your exciting journey through this wonderful new stage of life!

Index

Power of attorney 13, 129, 135, 137, 168
Pre-tax rate of return 49
Principal residence 45, 55, 88, 89, 90, 91, 92, 93, 94, 101, 153, 156, 157, 160, 163, 164
Private pension plan 40, 109

R

Rate of return 33, 35, 36, 39, 45, 47, 49, 57, 96, 98, 114, 115, 116, 117, 118, 124
Real estate 84, 85, 88, 91, 92, 93, 102, 146, 148, 156, 163
Real estate market 84, 85, 89
Red zone 118, 119, 123
Registered pension income 43
Registered retirement savings plan (RRSP) 40, 56, 57, 99, 101, 104, 108, 111, 113, 130, 155, 159, 163
Rental property income 40, 55, 87, 88, 90, 92
Reverse mortgage 56, 62, 63
Risk profile 12, 13, 39, 116, 121, 125, 126, 167, 168
RRIF 43, 44, 97, 101, 108, 143, 144, 155, 158, 159, 163

S

Scholarship 154
Seven critical risks 38, 42, 47, 52, 59

Severance payments 99
Sideways market 35
Spousal trust 145, 149
Standard deviation 36, 118, 119, 120
Stock 35, 107, 117, 161
Stock market 25, 36, 36, 39, 42, 61, 113, 114, 115, 116
Survivorship 141, 143, 149

T

Taxable assets 155
Taxable income 93, 97, 100, 101, 102, 103, 104, 107, 108, 130, 147, 157
Tax benefits 45, 131, 134, 159
Tax bracket 100, 147, 159
Tax credits 44, 96, 104, 105, 107, 111, 122, 134, 135, 136, 158
Tax deduction 104, 136
Tax efficiency 12, 13, 40, 45, 46, 49, 60, 63, 98, 99, 100, 107, 109, 110, 121, 124, 126, 152, 160, 168, 169
Tax efficient systematic withdrawal plan (TSWP) 45
Tax-free asset 152, 153
Tax-free benefit 130, 158
Tax-free capital gains 89
Tax-free equity 56
Tax-free income 93, 132
Tax-free savings account (TFSA) 40, 45, 153, 157, 159, 163, 164

Tax rate 44, 45, 47, 49, 93, 96, 97, 100, 101, 105, 106, 107, 110, 156
Tax saving 96, 104, 105, 159, 160
Tax zone 111
Testamentary trust 153, 159, 160, 161, 165
Transition 8, 9, 11, 18, 24, 31, 59, 153
Trust 88, 145, 149, 153, 159, 160, 161, 165,

U

U.S. Tax return 87, 88, 91

V

Volatility 30, 36, 37, 38, 39, 42, 117, 121, 122

W

Will 13, 129, 135, 137, 140, 144, 145, 148, 149, 151, 154, 158, 159, 160, 161, 162, 165, 168

Y

Yield 126

Bibliography

Canadian Census 2006

Canada's Aging Population 2002, Health Canada

7 Habits of Highly Effective People, Steven Covey, Free Press, 1989

Other Titles in
The Knowledge Bureau's
Master Your Series

MASTER
Your Taxes

How to maximize
your after-tax returns

Evelyn Jacks

FINANCIAL EDUCATION FOR DECISION MAKERS

MASTER
Your Money
Management

How to manage the advisors
who work for you

Jim Ruta BA, RHU

FINANCIAL EDUCATION FOR DECISION MAKERS